Romancing the $MOKE$TACK

HOW CITIES AND STATES PURSUE PROSPERITY

William Fulton

All of this material originally appeared in *Governing* magazine

ISBN: 0615395937
ISBN-13:978-0-61-539593-7

Published by
Solimar Books
P.O. Box 24618
Ventura, California 93002
www.cp-dr.com

For Allison

Table of Contents

Introduction

Twenty-five years ago, when I first started writing about economic development, the governors of seven states went on The Phil Donahue Show—the premiere daytime talk show of its time—and begged General Motors to build the assembly plant for its brand-new Saturn brand in their state. It was, to put it bluntly, a pretty pathetic excuse for an economic development campaign. Even though auto assembly plants don't literally have smokestacks, this was a pretty stark example of politicians trying to find a short-cut to economic success through the standard technique of "romancing the smokestack"—wooing some out-of-town business in hopes that they will come to town. I always counted the Donahue show as the lowest point in the history of American economic development—especially since none of the seven states got the plant.

At least the Donahue show *seemed* like the low point until earlier this year, when Ohio Gov. Ted Strickland made a Youtube music video begging basketball star LeBron James to re-sign with the Cleveland Cavaliers. The music video was even more of a low point that the Donahue episode because it managed to trivialize both the economic development goal and the means by which that goal is pursued. Somehow a talk show seems almost statesmanlike compared to a music video. And have we sunk so low that the holy grail of economic development is not an auto assembly plant but an individual basketball player? Not that it much mattered. In the end, making a music video didn't work any better than going on a talk show. The Saturn plant went to Tennessee—at least until GM killed the brand last year—and LeBron went to Florida.

If the humorous failures listed above teach us anything, it is this: There is no magic bullet for prosperity. You can't just romance the smokestack and hope to succeed, especially in the long run. But there are ways to maximize the chances of enduring success.

The fact that some communities are prosperous and some are not is hardly an accident. In large part, success is the result of deliberate effort on the part of business organizations, nonprofit entities such as research institutions and universities, and — yes — government agencies to nurture the growth and sustainability of particular businesses and particular types of economic activity in particular locations.

There's nothing new about this. For thousands of years, cities and regions have prospered when they have grabbed emerging economic opportunities and found ways to make sure the economic benefit flows toward them. Sometimes these efforts have been mostly private — as when the Columbian Rope Company, in the midst of the Depression, set up a research lab in my home town and hired my grandfather, a chemistry professor, to run it. Sometimes these have been mostly public — as when the Erie Canal was built by New York State and the interstate highway system was financed by the federal government. And sometimes these efforts have been a combination — as when Congress subsidized the private construction of the transcontinental railroad.

But in the last couple of decades, the activist role of local and regional players has become more evident. Silicon Valley is part of a worldwide economic elite largely because of the presence of Stanford University and the way entrepreneurs have leveraged Stanford's presence. Dallas and Denver are major cities largely because civic and political leaders built enormous airports — what one former Dallas mayor called "the port to the ocean of the air" — at a time when nobody else was doing so. Pittsburgh continues to prosper — despite the departure of its steel mills and a steady decline in population — because it has reinvented its economy over and over again.

These places are prosperous specifically because they have *not* tried to romance the smokestack into town. They know that prosperity isn't dependent on one company or one plant or one person. Prosperity — especially the kind that endures for decades — emerges from a carefully constructed ecosystem that nurtures and sustains skilled labor, innovative entrepreneurs, research breakthroughs, and well-capitalized start-ups. Such an ecosystem builds on the strengths that already exist in a city or a region or a state; and as it spins off wealth it plows a good portion of the profit back into the enterprise.

As the stories about the Saturn plant and LeBron James suggest, this kind of nurturing of the ecosystem is not always the popular image of economic development. Economic developers are sometimes viewed as the public-sector equivalent of corporate raiders, going around and stealing businesses from each other at the public's expense. At its worst, as this book shows, economic development really is no better than that. But at its best — as this book also shows — economic development is a miraculous thing to behold, as cities and states and universities and business organizations work together to take advantage of emerging opportunities and create enduring prosperity for a community and its people.

The 60-some-odd columns contained in this collection represent my contribution to the ongoing debate about economic development in the United States over the past 15 years, from 1995 through 2010. All of these columns originally appeared in *Governing* magazine, one of the nation's leading periodicals covering state and local government. Although each individual column is, by design, bite-sized, in the fullness of reading I think the columns reveal how economic development works — what a wide-ranging field it is, what's required to make it work, and why it so often doesn't work, at least not the way it's supposed to.

I first began writing this column in 1995, when Alan Ehrenhalt, *Governing*'s longtime editor, called me up and suggested that the column might be a way to "keep you in the magazine". I had been freelancing for *Governing* since it was founded in 1987, mostly on economic development issues. For a while the joke at *Governing* was that I was the "panacea editor," since my job was mostly to write lengthy articles about the latest economic development fad — auto assembly plants, convention centers, ballparks, entertainment-oriented downtowns — and prove that whatever I was writing about was not a panacea. To a certain extent, this has still been my job as the economic development columnist — though I have also used the space to highlight things I saw in my travels (nothing was ever more fun than the middle-of-the-night tour of the Federal Express operation at the Memphis Airport) and, often, things that were just plain counterintuitive (like the idea that China is losing manufacturing jobs just like we are).

With Alan's encouragement, I also tried to write as often as possible in a personal tone — drawing upon my own experiences and my own personal background. I always kept some personal details at a distance. For example, about halfway through the 15 years, I was elected to my local City Council. But I never revealed in the column that I had been elected to local office because I thought it would be a distraction from the overall point of the column. Nevertheless, certain personal themes kept coming back over and over again. I am surprised, for example, how often I have used my two geographical reference points — Upstate New York, where I grew up, and Southern California, where I have lived most of my adult life. These are the poles of my personal universe, of course, but they're also the perfect foils in writing about economic development — one cold, old, poor, and shrinking; the other warm, new, affluent, and growing.

Of course, my perspective changed dramatically over the 15 years that these columns were written. When I wrote my first column in the summer of 1995, I was a journalist and teacher, and my daughter was in kindergarten. I had spent most of my life observing and commenting, often at the 30,000-foot level. When I wrote the last column in this collection, more than 14 years later, I was a professional planning consultant and had just been sworn in as the mayor of my city, and my daughter was in college. In contrast to previous phases of my career, I now spend every minute of every day trying to make things happen on the ground. Obviously, I have a different view these days — less idealistic and less focused on sweeping trends; more pragmatic and more focused on the nuts and bolts of the everyday business of economic development. This shows in the way the column has evolved over time.

Through it all, however, I have never ceased to be fascinated by the process of how cities, regions, and states build prosperity and then how they maintain it over the long term. Great cities, large and small, are powered by great prosperity, and the smartest cities — just like the smartest businesses — understand that they have to continually plow the fruits of their prosperity into sustaining and reinventing themselves. It's a mysterious process, but, as I say, it's pretty miraculous when it works. Writing these columns helped unlock the mystery for me, at least somewhat. I hope that reading them does the same for you.

Producing this book — both the columns within it and the actual book itself — is an accomplishment that only came about with the assistance of many other people. I am greatly indebted to Alan Ehrenhalt for asking me to write the column in the first place, and all of the editors at *Governing* — especially John Martin and Penny Lemov — for assisting me over the years. Paul Shigley has provided me with matchless support and collaboration for many years. Special thanks to Robin Andersen for doing lots of little things that helped make this book possible and Jennifer Choi for proofreading it. Most of all, thanks to Allison Joe for her love and support and also for dreaming up an endless number of titles until she found the one that seemed right.

Bill Fulton
Ventura, California
September 2010

Luring

The Giveaway

The California beach town where I live is at war. But not with Japan or Iraq or even the federal government. We are at war with two neighboring cities, each less than 10 miles away.

For decades, these cities were intimidated by our Maginot Line of retail establishments — a regional mall, a half-dozen significant shopping centers and hundreds of small, locally owned businesses selling everything from running shoes to darts. Recently, however, the neighboring cities have figured out how to slip around our Maginot Line. They have spent the past several years providing tax abatements and other incentives to various businesses, and as a result they have amassed impressive weaponry along the freeway near our border: auto dealerships, outlet malls, movie theaters and, most devastating, that nuclear bomb of retailers, a Wal-Mart.

The result? Our town has lost its once-impressive lead in sales-tax revenues, and our regional mall has been decimated. Now our city manager is busy devising a counterattack. But, as in all arms races, the winners are losing as well. Both neighboring cities are teetering on the brink of insolvency because of all the subsidies they have proffered to the retailers. So while our mayor gets hammered for not doling out enough goodies to lure the retailers, the other two mayors get hammered for literally giving away the store.

In short, we are engaged in a classic economic development war. These wars are fought constantly all over the country. Governors line up to pay tribute to visiting Asian auto manufacturers who might build a plant in their state. Otherwise-proud mayors bow down in front of wealthy oafs who happen to own sports teams. Armies of bureaucrats struggle to show how much prospective tax revenue they can yield to the captains of industry in order to keep them or lure them.

It is a sordid and depressing war, one decried on a regular basis by everyone from the president on down. We are impoverishing our communities through foolish tax giveaways, the argument goes. The library has no money because of the tax abatements we gave to the big chain bookstore. Tax abatements are shifting the load from businesses to average homeowners who can ill afford this added burden. Wouldn't it be better if we all just worked together and left this petty bickering behind?

All this is true enough. But it ignores one important fact. Competition for economic growth is undeniably, irrevocably American — and therefore unavoidable. In many ways, the whole history of the United States is the history of communities competing with each other. In the 19th century, the federal government encouraged the willy-nilly creation of communities in the Midwest and West as a means of dispersing the population from the crowded East and South. And the results were wonderfully American. Western towns were platted on paper and sold to unwitting customers in the East even before they were built. Every aspiring Midwestern town started a college — not for culture or education, but to attract people and businesses — and in the process they changed the very nature of higher education. Civic boosters created cities such as Houston, Dallas and Los Angeles out of little more than dirt and dreams. The driving force behind the growth of American communities — and America itself — was not theology or vision or culture or even commerce, but salesmanship.

There is a difference, however, between building a port and subsidizing a Wal-Mart. And therein lies the sadness of today's economic development efforts.

A port — or a college or an airport — enriches a community. Such pieces of economic infrastructure are often financially stupid decisions, at least in the short run. But their tide of red ink often leaves a wake of energy and momentum that eventually pays off. Denver International Airport may seem troubled and expensive and remote today, but 50 years from now it will be viewed as visionary.

A tax giveaway, however, enriches only the corporation that receives it. Tax abatements may keep a plant or a store open for a few years. But business is business, and local governments can't control all the forces — markets, pricing, competition, even currency fluctuation — that affect a private company's decision to close a store or a plant.

A half-century from now, the state university currently being built in our county will be a well-established part of our landscape. So will the commercial airport people are beginning to think must be created after our local military base closes. Some people think these institutions aren't a good idea — that they might create a cycle of growth that will spiral out of control. That may be. But they're probably a better foundation for our future than the Wal-Mart, the auto dealerships and the outlet malls — all of which will probably be gone, leaving only political divisiveness and economic ruin in their wake.

1995

The Smokestack Chase

When Don Jakeway took over as Ohio's economic development director six years ago, he decided that just pulling in companies and holding press conferences wasn't enough. Working for Republican Governor George V. Voinovich, Jakeway wanted to make the whole system more accountable — so that the state could measure success more readily, and make sure that the companies were rewarded for doing the right thing, not for threatening to move out of the state.

Today, Jakeway presides over an unusual employment tax credit program that is nothing if not accountable. The credit on state income taxes is not fixed; it varies depending on the type and pay scale of the job, as well as the socioeconomic profile of the worker.Jakeway works with the state's income tax collectors to double-check company reporting. And instead of up-front subsidies, companies get tax credits only for those new jobs they actually create. "If you don't create a job," Jakeway says, "you don't get the incentive."

The Ohio program is just one example of the latest trend in economic development programs around the country. It's not enough anymore for the governor to hold a photo op at the site of the new factory and say that a thousand jobs are going to be created. Now, both governors and their economic development directors are under pressure to be accountable. They want to prove that the tax breaks they're giving away actually make a difference in company location decisions, and to follow up and make sure that the promised jobs are actually created. Indeed, governors in several states have set up blue-ribbon commissions to examine the effectiveness of economic development programs.

The accountability trend is driven partly by conservative state legislators, whose small-government ideology is causing them to question something that looks suspiciously like left-wing "industrial policy." And in part, it's driven by the need, resulting from ever- tighter fiscal conditions, to reassess government spending of all types. Hence, economic development programs — long accepted as a political necessity, at the very least — are under the microscope for the first time.

All this is a big change from how economic development has worked historically — especially big-time economic development, in which mayors and governors have played a game of high-stakes poker with company CEOs. In that environment, all that mattered was the number of jobs that got into the headline; the pressure on politicians and economic developers were to push the numbers as high as possible, no matter how much truth was in them. "In general, they go after everything that flies," quips William Schweke, program director at the Corporation for Enterprise Development, "and claim everything that lands."

The accountability trend has forced a lot of economic developers to document what they're up to for the first time. This, in turn, has led to a sharpening of program goals and objectives. For example, economist Timothy Bartik of the Upjohn Institute in Michigan argues that most economic development programs simply don't pay for themselves in increased tax receipts. But they still can be worthwhile investments if they bring in jobs and improve the general economic health of the region or state. "Too many people still think of economic development as a fiscal game, not an employment game," he says. With more accountability, the fiscal argument is likely to be "shaken out" of the program's goals if it's bogus — and then politicians can debate the pros and cons of the program based on its impact on the labor market.

Of course, accountability — or, at least, supposedly objective measurement of success — may not really be all it's cracked up to be. Many experts are suspicious of the numbers companies report. "Only the company knows how much [of a tax break] is enough," says Schweke. If a state official asks a company CEO if the tax break from the governor helped keep the company in the state — well, how many CEOs are going to say no?

And there's no question that sometimes politicians don't really want to know whether the deal they're pursuing is worth it. The accountability trend is littered with discarded data that show some particular incentive was a loser — but it was chosen because the mayor or the governor, finger to the political winds, decided it was a winner. Overall, accountability probably will bring more political credibility to economic development, if only by defusing the notion that economic developers are plaid-jacket giveaway artists who will make a deal at any cost. Of course, accountability might actually help create better public policy in the economic development area as well. But, clearly, that would be a bonus.

1996

The Subsidized Job Shuffle

Sometimes the federal government concocts so many different ways of trying to help a community that it's hard to know which of them, if any, is having an effect. This is a problem in virtually every policy area, but it's especially frustrating in economic development, where almost every federal department has at least one major program designed to promote local economic prosperity. Meaningful evaluations are a rarity.

Now, however, the U.S. General Accounting Office (GAO) has given us something of a road map. In a recent report, the GAO provides an overview of eight major federal programs dealing with economic development activities — programs run by no less than seven different federal agencies.

The report is a first cut at understanding how federal economic development funds are really used. In particular, the GAO sought to delineate whether federal funds were being deployed in some cases simply to relocate businesses and jobs from one area to another. This is an important question, because local economic development officials are frequently criticized for wasting federal money on what amounts to rearranging the deck chairs of their metropolitan economies, with no overall gain in economic activity.

For example, if federal funds are used to subsidize the move of an industrial company from the Frost Belt to the Sun Belt — or from the inner city to the greener pastures of the suburbs — is that really economic development? A mayor or governor whose community happens to benefit may well say yes, but from a regional or national point of view, the answer is not so clear.

The GAO found that three of the eight programs have an outright prohibition on use of federal funds to relocate jobs. But Economic Development Administration infrastructure grants, Empowerment Zone money and federal job-training funds account for only about 8 percent of the $15.7 billion a year that the eight programs as a group dole out. For the other 92 percent — more than $14 billion a year — there is no similar restriction.

Furthermore, almost all of the 92 percent is contained in three big-ticket federal programs: Community Development Block Grants (run by the Department of Housing and Urban Development), revolving loans under the Clean Water Act (administered by the Environmental Protection Agency) and funds available under the Surface Transportation Program (operated by the Department of Transportation). These three programs each deliver more than $4 billion a year to American communities. Together, they account for more than 80 percent of federal economic development spending. And there is no federal restriction on using these funds for zero-sum job relocation.

Do these statistics mean that a massive amount of federal money is being used simply to move jobs around? Not necessarily. Responding to criticism from several federal agencies, the Commerce Department in particular, the GAO says it has no proof that relocations are being subsidized with federal funds — merely that, in most cases, such relocations are not prohibited.

One way to respond to the GAO data would be to cry "foul" and insist that a blanket prohibition on job relocation be included in all federal programs. Some members of Congress will undoubtedly lean toward doing that. But it would be a little simplistic.

It's true that there's no overarching federal policy on job relocation, or even on the ultimate goals of federal economic development programs. Yet buried within each program is a set of assumptions about what the geographical result should be — and here, perhaps, is where a useful discussion about the federal impact can begin.

For example: Community Development Block Grants (CDBG) contain no restriction on relocating jobs. But CDBGs generally must be spent in distressed neighborhoods. So, if CDBGs are used to relocate jobs from prosperous areas to poor ones, is this necessarily a bad thing? And how can local communities coordinate their efforts if CDGB money can be used to relocate jobs to poor neighborhoods but Empowerment Zone money cannot?

Meanwhile, the Surface Transportation Program takes a completely different approach. While it doesn't prohibit job relocation, the transportation program does encourage spending on mass transit, which presumably helps central cities. Instead of dictating a policy outcome, the transportation program leaves most spending decisions up to regional planning agencies — which necessarily reflect the political consensus in each metropolitan area.

It's hard to say what the best approach is. But it's safe to bet that simply asking whether jobs are relocated with federal funds is the wrong way to approach the discussion. Sometimes relocating jobs might be a good thing; other times it might be a bad thing. Or the same job relocation might be a good thing in Minneapolis but a bad thing in Miami. The GAO report gives us a hint of what the combined federal impact is. Now we need to have an informed discussion of what it ought to be.

1998

The Endless Subsidy Cycle

Gloria Whisenhunt is mad. And while her anger is unlikely to alter the history of American government, it may well serve as a warning shot for politicians and economic development practitioners who are a little too quick with the cash.

Whisenhunt is a hairdresser from Forsyth County, North Carolina, where Winston-Salem is located. In 1996, after six years as a county school board member, she won election to the Forsyth County board of commissioners. The very first item on which she had to vote, she recalls, was a request from the local economic development organization asking the county to pay for the infrastructure serving a new industrial park. The county had to bear the cost, she and her fellow commissioners were told, because otherwise Forsyth County would be at a competitive disadvantage with other communities around the South that were paying such costs.

Reluctantly, she voted in favor of the payment, hoping that would be the end of it. But it wasn't. A short time later, the economic development specialists were back — this time asking the county to provide a cash subsidy to the first business seeking to move into the industrial park. She balked, and again the specialists insisted that if Forsyth did not take this step, the county would be placed in a competitive disadvantage. This time, she said no. As a small-business owner, she believed that giving subsidies to some businesses and not others wasn't fair. Also, she didn't see where or how the endless cycle of subsidies would stop. "I didn't feel like I was doing what I should be doing for existing taxpayers," says Whisenhunt.

And so Gloria Whisenhunt began a crusade to implement the economic development equivalent of a non-proliferation treaty. She drafted a model resolution that was passed by her colleagues on the Forsyth County board of commissioners. The resolution states the county's desire to eliminate cash subsidies to businesses for economic development purposes, and it commits the county to such a course of action — if most other local governments in the Southeast do so as well.

Whisenhunt soon began stumping the conventions of the county officials to encourage others to do the same. "Most communities publicly express their disapproval of incentives, yet many also admit to feeling addicted to the process," she would say in her stump speech. "Often, it is the smaller counties which have had some recent success with incentives that are the most reluctant to kick the habit." Her crusade got a lot of attention, not only in North Carolina but in economic development circles around the country.

The story of Gloria Whisenhunt would seem little more than a colorful yarn about a local commissioner tilting at windmills except for the fact that it came at a time when North Carolinians were debating the merits of economic incentives to lure prosperous businesses into specific locations around the state. Last year, after a vigorous debate, the legislature approved a law granting tax breaks to two businesses seeking to build new plants. Nucor Corp., a Charlotte-based steel company, received about $160 million in tax credits and tax exemptions for building a recycling plant in Hertford County, a rural area in northeastern North Carolina. And Federal Express received $115 million for building a sorting hub in Guilford County between Greensboro and Winston-Salem. The Nucor plant delivered 300 jobs, the FedEx hub 1,500.

The Nucor/FedEx deal was not the first piece of legislation in North Carolina permitting state and local tax breaks for economic development, but it was the most important. The resulting subsidies were sizable indeed. FedEx is one of America's most successful companies, yet the state was giving the company more than $76,000 per job. And the price tag for Nucor was more than a half-million dollars per job — a figure that exceeds even many of the sweetheart auto-plant deals of the 1980s and represents a big shift for a state that had resisted playing the smokestack-chasing game in recent years.

So, just as Gloria Whisenhunt suggested in her stump speech, a lot of North Carolina legislators played the issue both ways. They expressed concern about providing financial incentives to private companies — and then voted for the bill. Now that the bill has passed, North Carolina localities (especially rural ones) will have far more freedom to lure companies with tax breaks.

All of this means that Commissioner Whisenhunt is angrier than ever. So far, she's gotten very few takers on her non-proliferation idea. But the mere fact that she has been able to get so much publicity suggests that the spiraling trend toward economic development incentives has taken a toll on our state and local political system. And in that may lie the beginning of the end for ill-considered tax- incentive giveaways.

1999

The Job Hunt

One of my mentors, the late Cornell planning professor K.C. Parsons, used to have a succinct two-word description for the business of economic development. He called it "buying jobs."

In depressed Upstate New York, where he taught and where I grew up, he wasn't wrong. As long ago as the 1950s, when a factory threatened to leave, the towns began to pony up subsidies: free land, free buildings, tax rebates. If the subsidy got deep enough, the company stayed. If we were outbid by the aggressive, no-union Carolinas, the company left.

In time, the game stopped working. Not only were New York and Massachusetts outbid by Carolina, but Carolina was outbid by Texas, and then Texas was outbid by Mexico and Latin America. No amount of subsidy in the world could compete with low wages. This was good in a certain way. It forced the Northern cities to face the reality of economic transformation, and it began building a middle class in low-wage locations such as Mexico.

But now America's Northern and Southern cities are in the same boat when it comes to manufacturing jobs, and the fledgling Mexican middle class is being undercut by China, Eastern Europe and other parts of Asia. One of the reasons Wal-Mart, the world's largest company, has come to be vilified is because its business model is based on the worldwide "race to the bottom." Goods are made by the lowest-paid workers in the world and then sold by the lowest-paid workers in the United States. Americans love a bargain, but we also love to hate the business owners who make the bargains possible. The two-tier economy seems more of a reality in the America of today than it has in almost a century.

These days, other middle-class service jobs are also getting shipped overseas — even ones that used to be required for local businesses. The biggest medical group in my town now ships dictation to India every night when the doctors go home — and has transcriptions back the next morning by the time the doctors arrive at the office. Indians are well educated, they speak English and the 12-hour time difference is perfect.

In many cases, the tax system works against the creation of middle- class jobs. In the beachfront area of California where I now live, the game is to buy tax revenue, not jobs, and that only fuels the two-tiered economy. It's bad enough that the median home price is more than $500,000, and the average retail wage is $25,000 a year. On top of that, California's Proposition 13-driven tax system has created low property taxes and placed cities in competition for sales taxes. There is a clear cause and effect here. Local officials have every motivation to stimulate creation of more high-end houses and more retail stores with low-end jobs, and that very simply is because those are the two things that bring in tax revenue.

Maybe the United States will become one big Holland, living off of its investments around the world or — at least in a place such as coastal California — one big Monaco where the rich play and somehow find a place to house the people they need to provide them with service. For individual communities and the economic development practitioners who serve them, however, this creates a tough dilemma with moral dimensions. Maybe economic development is still a business of buying jobs, but which jobs? At what price? Can good jobs be retained when the world is engaged in a race to the bottom? And are the bad ones you can get worth the cost? In other words, is it okay to buy into the two-tiered economy and get as much of it as you can? Or should you try to bend that trend to benefit your town?

There's an assumption embedded in economic development — indeed, in the whole business of American community-building — that we citizens can control our destiny. It's part of the whole can-do approach in the United States: If we have a vision, and we can muster the resources, we can do anything. We may need the help of our state or federal government, or we might need to create business or civic alliances, but nevertheless there is a sense that if we put our minds and bodies to the task, we can achieve just about anything. Somewhere in the world there is money, there are natural resources, and there are markets. If we can find all those things and put them together in the right way, our communities can succeed.

Even in the context of the global race to the bottom, this is still true. We can understand markets, we can understand money, we put things together to get the best possible result. But it's disconcerting to think that the best possible result might not be as good as it used to be. For those who can afford a million-dollar house, or who can somehow have a satisfying life on $12 an hour, maybe things will be okay. But for the rest of us, the standard economic development formula may not work anymore.

2004

Learning

Getting The Job Done

Fifteen years ago, the so-called "Massachusetts miracle" created a high-tech boom that lifted a long-languishing Northeastern state out of the economic doldrums. Now, however, Massachusetts has a different kind of problem: not enough workers. In the past decade, the national labor force expanded by 11 percent. But Massachusetts' supply of labor increased only 1.5 percent — less than one-seventh of the national total.

Dig deeper, though, and you'll find that Massachusetts' real problem isn't a lack of workers. Rather, it's a lack of workers who can do the jobs the economy is creating. Because, like so many other parts of the country, one thing that Massachusetts isn't lacking is fresh blood. In the past decade, the state added more than 300,000 people. That's a 5 percent increase — not a huge number but a healthy one. Virtually the entire net increase in the state's population came from immigration.

The Hispanic population rose by half; the Asian population went up 67 percent.

Many of these immigrants, of course, have little education and few skills. So they're stuck in dead-end jobs, while the high end of the economy can't find the workers required for the jobs being created .

And they're concentrated in central cities. (According to one recent study, 48 percent of Massachusetts' foreign-born residents live in central cities, compared with 30 percent of native-born residents.) So it's become good politics in urban Massachusetts to advocate "skills training" for immigrant groups, even if the skills are pretty basic.

Boston Mayor Thomas Menino recently hosted a "skills summit" for the Northeast, partly to tout a program encouraging literacy and English proficiency that's being funded by developer fees. And the Massachusetts Institute for a New Commonwealth (MassINC), a think tank, is pushing adult literacy as the key in the state's economic growth. One in three Massachusetts workers lacks necessary job skills, MassINC reports. That's 1 million people overall, including almost 700,000 who have high school diplomas. The MassINC study throws around terms such as "Adult Basic Education," to distinguish it from the traditional university extension and field-trips-for-seniors orientation of adult education.

Developer fees spent on literacy? Adult education as the key to prosperity? What's going on?

Welcome to the 21st century, where all those sports stadiums, convention centers and high-profile headquarters don't matter nearly so much as the prosaic nuts and bolts of helping people get and keep jobs. The key to the future of the American economy is linking people to skills and skilled workers to jobs. And there's only one growing source of potential skilled labor: the mostly unskilled and poorly educated immigrants from Asia and Latin America who are now living in our nation's central cities. Hence, literacy programs instead of convention centers.

It's refreshing to view immigration as a work-force issue rather than a social services issue, which is how it usually gets cast in the public policy debate. Indeed, in the past year or two, the entire economic development policy debate in the United States has shifted.

It now centers on the emerging multi-ethnic work force. And we're not talking just about mid-career retooling for laid-off factory workers.

Increasingly, we're seeing a focus on basic literacy training and work-force skills. This trend even moves into the debate on urban and regional planning, where some "work-force development" component is becoming standard. Indeed, the battle over "affordable housing" is no longer, by and large, a clash over where to put poor people. In our largest metro area, it's become a debate about where and how to build houses and apartments for our emerging work force.

And the whole issue of work-force assistance for America's emerging population is only going to become a bigger issue in politics in the future. Antonio Villaraigosa may have lost the recent Los Angeles mayoral election to James Hahn (who had a white-black coalition), but there is little doubt that a Villaraigosa-style campaign appealing to these new populations will succeed at some point in the future. And the politics of work-force assistance will increasingly play well in the older suburbs, too, which are quickly changing to become more multiethnic.

Of course, we've been through this before — with the forebears of those Americans who see the economic future in sports stadiums and convention centers. The urban politics of the 19th century encouraged the upward mobility of the European immigrants of that era. Once the upward mobility started, so did the demand for suburban housing and metropolitan amenities of the sort that more recent economic development-types like to promote. So it makes sense that the new urban ethnic coalitions will take on economic development issues in the service of upward mobility. If they succeed, perhaps in 20 years we'll be subsidizing soccer stadiums.

2001

Reversing The Brain Drain

My daughter is in high school, but she is spending the summer attending our local community college — getting a leg up on her advanced high school courses and maybe college as well. There's no telling what she'll do when college time rolls around in two years, but one scenario goes like this: She goes to the community college — free.

That's because the nonprofit foundation supporting our local community college now pays all tuition and fees for any resident of my town who goes there. The main goal is social equity: to make sure that all kids in our town have access to college no matter the family income. But there's an important economic development goal as well: to train local kids for local jobs and, just as important, try to get the kids to stick around.

Institutions of higher learning have always played an important role in the economic growth of communities. They are stable employers, rooted in the community; they have jobs of all kinds; and they pay good wages. In addition, they attract college-age migrants who by definition are highly educated and often decide to stay in town. In the best of all worlds — Silicon Valley, for example — the graduates create successful spin-off businesses that drive the local economy.

Recently, however, we've seen a new twist on this old theme: scholarships designed not to attract college students from elsewhere but to get promising young people to stay put.

The scholarship program at my local community college is one example. Our California beach town has very high housing prices and a lot of low-wage jobs, meaning that kids looking for mid-level jobs — machinists, nurses, entry-level office workers — go elsewhere to live. The theory is that if they can get training for mid-level jobs locally, they'll make more contacts and decide to stay. It's a way to stem the brain drain.

In other parts of the country, the brain drain is a much more serious problem because college-age kids perceive so little economic opportunity. And so the efforts to counteract the brain drain have to be much more aggressive.

Perhaps the best example in the Rust Belt these days is Kalamazoo, an aging and struggling industrial Michigan city. Its economy and population are flat, while suburban flight continues. The result is very little demand for housing or anything else in the city itself.

At least that was the result until a group of local philanthropists got together with the city school district to create the Kalamazoo Promise. Now, any student who enters the city school system no later than 9th grade gets a college scholarship — 100 percent for kids who've been in Kalamazoo their whole lives, 65 percent for those who move there for high school. Half of the city's 472 June graduates will get a free college ride, but there's a geographical catch: They get the scholarship only if they go to a state-supported public university or community college in Michigan.

The benefit is twofold. Kalamazoo kids stay in the state for college, and Kalamazoo creates a market for residents. A large homebuilder in the state is now focusing more attention on the city, hoping to build homes for families interested in the Kalamazoo Promise.

Some folks in the Rust Belt believe that keeping their kids at home isn't possible. School administrators in the Northeast and Midwest often say that the best they can hope for is to make sure local kids get a decent education before they move away. But giving a financial break for a geographical preference is an old idea in education — and a successful one. In fact, I took advantage of it twice — on opposite sides of the country.

When I graduated from high school in New York State, I received a Regents Scholarship — worth $250 per year — that was redeemable only inside the state. The Regents Scholarship more than offset my community college costs, and when I went away to a four-year private university, I defrayed the cost by using the same scholarship. That kept me in the state for the first part of my working career.

Later, after I had established residency in California, I took advantage of the famous in-state tuition break to get a graduate degree at the University of California at a fraction of its market value. That education and the contacts I made getting it have kept me in California ever since.

I don't know where my daughter will decide to go to college, but I do know that the combination of price and geography will be a factor.

2006

The Case For Technical Education

When I was a kid in the 1960s and 70s, I was an anomaly on my block: Both my parents had gone to college. They both had managed to make it through small liberal arts universities during the Great Depression, when something like 6 percent of all Americans had college degrees. Most of my friends had one parent, at most, who went to college. In many cases, no one in the family had ever made it past high school.

The funny thing was that even though our family was more highly educated than most in our little factory town, we weren't better off. My father sold cars and my mother worked part-time at a nursery school. The unionized shop workers whose families I knew generally made more money, had better benefits and enjoyed more job security than my parents did. That's because in those days — the height of America's industrial era — the path to economic security did not lead to college. It led to unionized factory jobs.

All that went out the window when the plants shut down, not only in my hometown but all over the country. The semi-skilled factory job was no longer a path to the future; it was a road to nowhere. Many in my generation heard — and took to heart — the ubiquitous phrase, "To get a good job, get a good education." To us, that meant one thing: Get a four-year academic degree and get away from the factory.

But what is a good education? And what kind of good education will lead to a good job? Forty years after my generation grappled with it, this question is being revisited — especially with President Obama's emphasis on strengthening community colleges. And the answer appears to be this: Academic learning still matters, but it's not enough. To get a good job, a lot of people need a good technical education as well. They need to have practical, problem-solving knowledge that they can put to use in the real world.

There are still factory jobs around — 10 percent of all American jobs are in manufacturing — but factory workers today are highly skilled employees who work in a fast-paced environment where they have to be able to think on their feet. The same is true in what might be considered the factories of the service economy — hospitals, for example, where nurses and their aides must make decisions in real time that could have life-or-death results.

Even America's innovation factories — the research institutions that generate new products — require highly skilled personnel with technical training, not just the research superstars that everybody's always talking about. For example, at Amgen, the largest biotech company in the world and also the largest private employer in the county where I now live, supports the fact that it takes many skilled lab technicians to support each superstar researcher.

These are the kinds of good-paying jobs that the American economy is growing fast. Meanwhile, conventional white-collar jobs, such as clerical, accounting, even legal — the "good jobs" that the old slogan referred to — are going overseas.

In other words, the path to economic security no longer leads to college — at least not the traditional four-year college that was supposed to deliver you to a white-collar job. The path to economic security, especially for the working class and children of immigrants, leads to a community college, where you can get a combination of academic education and technical training — life skills and jobs skills.

Yet the academic education that produces white-collar workers remains highly valued, while the technical education that offers people the knowledge and skills to take the new jobs is still looked down upon. Major state universities get lots of money; community colleges, which provide most of the technical training, don't. This may be a vestige of the 1970s, or it may simply be the result of the fact that virtually all people involved in higher education themselves are products of the white-collar, four-year-degree factories.

Obama's emphasis on community colleges is welcome, but money remains an issue. Given the struggles that states have today, it's hard to imagine how they can give priority to both major research universities and community colleges. Increasingly, big employers, frustrated that the public education system can't deliver the workers they need, actually are funding technical education through community colleges. Bluegrass Community College, for example, has a campus on the grounds of Toyota's big assembly plant in Georgetown, Kentucky. As a technical training center, it looks a lot more like a factory floor than it does a conventional classroom.

The future of education will probably look more like Toyota's idea of a classroom than a state university's idea. Or at least it ought to — if American educators follow the economy and focus on technical education as well as academic learning.

2009

Branding

The Pov-Prof Mystique

Not long ago, the woman who gives me my morning caffeine at my local coffee shop announced that I would be on my own from now on. "I'm giving this up," she said. "I've decided it's time to create my jewelry full-time."

Since I'm an urban planner by training, the immediate question that came to my mind was not what kind of jewelry she'd be making, but WHERE she would be making and selling it. "I'm going to rent a place over on The Avenue," she answered. "That's the place to be."

In my town of Ventura, California, "The Avenue" is the colloquial term people use for an older neighborhood located near our downtown business district. Once the local center of heavy industry, it is now a mixed and mostly Latino neighborhood. But because it's diverse, cheap and "funky," it also has become the local art colony, with artists of all kinds renting space to make and sell their merchandise.

The influx of these artists — and the organizations that they are bringing with them — has had a major impact on The Avenue. It's revived the local economy. It's created some cross-cultural connections in the community that didn't previously exist. And it's brought people from other parts of town and even from distant parts of the region into a neighborhood that most of them used to avoid like the plague.

The Avenue, it turns out, is not so unusual in this regard. In fact, it's what Mark Stern and Susan Seifert, economic development researchers at the University of Pennsylvania, call a classic "pov- prof" neighborhood — a neighborhood with a higher-than-usual presence of both poor people and professionals. In the past couple of decades, these neighborhoods have been viewed mainly as areas of social strife: Gentrifiers drive up rents — thus reviving the area — but in the process drive the poor people out. According to Stern and Seifert, however, the pov-prof neighborhoods are actually playing a critical economic role, connecting otherwise isolated areas to the economy of entire metropolitan regions.

In their recent "Social Impact of the Arts" project, Stern and Seifert took a detailed look at geographical patterns surrounding arts and cultural activities in Philadelphia and other cities across the country. And what they found was a fascinating dichotomy. These activities — and the organizations required to organize and run them — have come to be disproportionately located in the pov-prof neighborhoods. But the people who attend the regular cultural events come from a much wider area — indeed, from all over the region.

In Philadelphia, Stern and Seifert found cultural and artistic activity to be concentrated mostly in pov-prof neighborhoods near Center City and in west and northwest Philadelphia. But fully 80 percent of the people who participated in the events came from somewhere else.

This is an extraordinary finding, especially in a hyper-segregated city like Philadelphia, where the geography of race plays a dominant role in almost everybody's daily activities, whether they are white or black. Despite the inevitable cultural and racial divisions, it turns out that cultural institutions thrive in diverse neighborhoods. And these institutions attract people from all over. "There is a regional audience for community arts," says Stern. "Arts and cultural activities are geographically bounded. But the audience is not."

The lesson in all this for economic development is pretty obvious. Finding effective ways to stimulate economic activity in transitional neighborhoods has always been a difficult task. But arts and culture appear to be one area of human endeavor in which the patrons — the people who bring in the money — expect diversity and funkiness and are in fact willing to search it out. In the research they did for "Social Impact of the Arts," Stern and Seifert found the same pattern of activity in many other cities, including Chicago and San Francisco.

It's not certain that the diversity being created in the pov-prof neighborhoods in question is going to be permanent. The old gentrification issue still exists — if an artsy area becomes successful, it's possible that the rents will rise too high for the povs to pay, and they will be forced to move out. Increasingly, however, the profs and the povs seem to want to work together to maintain a neighborhood's delicate balance. Programs linking artists with minority children in these neighborhoods, for example, are on the rise — and some of them are showing impressive results.

Effective economic development often turns out to be a matter of finding the right niche. And that means finding reasons why lots of different people might want to converge on a particular place. For distinctive big-city downtowns and for older, affluent suburbs, this has rarely been a problem. But for transitional urban neighborhoods, arts and culture may be one way to stimulate economic growth — and new experiments in civic participation to boot.

1999

Playing Off History

The Erie Canal was the mother of all economic development projects — costly, controversial and ultimately successful in transforming both the economic and natural landscape of its time and place. While the canal was being built two centuries ago, it was viewed as outrageously expensive and perhaps even unnecessary. Only a half-century or so after it was completed in 1825, railroads made canals obsolete. But by then, the canal had altered the economics of the whole region forever.

In the process of cutting a 300-mile swath of waterways, locks and tow paths across the wilderness of Upstate New York, the Erie Canal laid the foundation for an economic landscape that remains distinctive to this day. Cities and towns sprang up to serve the canal all the way from Albany to Buffalo. Many of them were subsequently transformed into 20th-century factory towns, but many more still remain largely as they were in the 19th century, with "Canal Street" meandering downhill toward the old warehouses along the banks of what some have called the "artificial river."

Even as the economic landscape has remained, however, the economy that created it is long gone. Once the major thoroughfare for goods in the entire world, the canal route is now outside the economic mainstream — left behind in a world shaped by air travel and automobiles. So it's more than a little ironic that politicians and economic development specialists in Upstate New York have recently come to see this charming but non-functioning landscape as the possible foundation for an economic revival.

In the past decade, the New York State government and the federal government have committed hundreds of millions of dollars to projects designed to encourage recreation and tourism along the Erie Canal route. The idea is that in today's economy, upstate's cultural history is the region's greatest asset — especially for the hundreds of small towns along the canal route that lie between big cities such as Albany, Syracuse, Rochester and Buffalo.

The canal revival effort has taken many forms. Much of the work on recreational tourism has been undertaken by the New York State Canal Corp., a subsidiary of the Thruway Authority. Many economic development projects in towns have been underwritten by the U.S. Department of Housing and Urban Development — in large part because HUD Secretary Andrew Cuomo, who might run for governor of New York someday, found the idea attractive.

Many of the projects being undertaken will undoubtedly be successful on their own terms. A major effort to provide consistent and informative "wayfinding signs" will surely help. And plans to attract boating recreationists to the canal have a good chance of success as well. The Finger Lakes region contains the highest concentration of recreational boats in all of New York State, yet only a few of them find their way onto the canal even though it is connected to the lakes.

But the bigger question is whether the people of Upstate New York will truly embrace the notion that their region is best used as a kind of vast cultural museum. As an upstate native, I personally have no problem with this proposition. But, coming from a small factory town, I also recognize that this represents a huge shift in the way people there think about the place that they call home.

"Upstate New York has been a `production landscape' — working factories and farms," says Karen Engelke of the Mohawk Valley Heritage Commission, which has worked with many communities on canal-related revival. "We have traditionally held the view that what happens between 6 a.m. and 6 p.m. is what's most important. Now, we have to accustom ourselves to thinking of our area as a 'presentation landscape.'"

The shift is far from impossible, of course. New England has made the transition very successfully. So have certain other parts of Upstate New York, most notably Cooperstown, which houses not just the Baseball Hall of Fame but also the Farmers Museum, the Glimmerglass Opera and a whole slew of attractions related to the work of James Fenimore Cooper.

When I was a kid, I used to travel to Cooperstown with my Great-Great Aunt Nell, who had lived down the road ever since she was born, back in the 1870s. She always made a beeline straight for the Hall of Fame and shunned the Farmers Museum. The reason? She loved baseball — the Dodgers were her favorite team — and she had little interest in 19th- century plows. "Oh, I used all that stuff," she always said. In other words, she was just too close to what I considered "history" to think it was interesting on its own terms.

For the entire 20th century, upstaters viewed canal towns the same way. But now, in the 21st century, maybe they'll have enough distance from the history around them to view their landscape as an asset, even if it no longer produces anything.

2000

Hyping The Hip

Should cities be cool or uncool? If they need to be cool, do they make that happen with art galleries and restaurants? Or with sports stadiums?

A few years ago, Richard Florida — then a professor at Carnegie Mellon University — turned the world of economic development upside down with his book "The Rise of the Creative Class." Florida argued that the engine of the American economy is the highly educated group of people who create things — artists, scientists — that are then transformed into new products. Florida's argument has been widely interpreted to mean that cities, in order to attract this "creative class," must provide a whole range of hip and cool amenities, including bars, restaurants and art galleries.

Florida's ideas have hatched a whole new generation of intellectuals articulating the value of creativity in economic development. Witness the recent hullabaloo in New York, for example, over the publication of "The Warhold Economy," by Florida protege Elizabeth Currid, which manages to combine hip, on-the-scene descriptions of the New York art scene with sober analysis of the role that the arts play in the city's economy. And the Florida view also has led to a whole new generation of economic development practice, which is focused on developing the urban amenities that Florida's creative class supposedly desires.

Not surprisingly, the cool-cities trend has led to a counter-trend, both intellectually and in practice, that advocates the deliberate creation and nurturing of uncool cities. The most public advocate of the uncool city is Joel Kotkin, the often contrarian commentator on cities and economic development. Kotkin has always been a defender of what he calls "nerdistans": boring suburbs that nevertheless house some of the most powerful drivers of the American economy, especially in the tech sectors. He has frequently argued that the decline of manufacturing in the United States is over-hyped, and more recently he has criticized rebuilding efforts in New Orleans for focusing on what he calls "the ephemeral city" — essentially, the bread and circuses of the creative class rather than the nuts and bolts of basic infrastructure.

So who's right? What's best for the American economy? Do cities need to be cool or uncool? They need to be both, because the economic processes that will sustain cities in the 21st century involve both.

Let's begin with the "creative class." Florida's basic argument has gotten a bit twisted in interpretation. He's not suggesting that arts and culture in themselves should be the basis for a city's entire economy and that therefore the entire point of economic development should be to nurture that sector of the economy. Rather, he's saying that a wide variety of urban amenities, including art and culture, are required to attract and retain a multiplicity of creative people — not just artists but research scientists, designers and all kinds of other people.

I think he's right. Not long ago, I was giving a speech in just about the most blue-collar city you can imagine — Buffalo — and I made the Florida argument. New York State was investing hundreds of millions of dollars in life sciences research in Buffalo in an effort to compete with Georgia, Arizona and California in this sector of huge economic opportunity. I pointed out that the prevalent new development pattern in Buffalo was the creation of three-acre suburban lots but that research scientists trying to cure cancer did not want to spend all weekend on a riding mower.

Afterwards, one woman came up to me and told me she works at a cancer research institute. "You're right," she said of the scientists. "At the end of the day, all they want is a restaurant, a gym and a loft."

Yet coolness alone will not make American cities work in the 21st century. The coolness must generate research breakthroughs, which must be pushed through the product development cycle and then manufactured and brought to market. Although manufacturing employment worldwide is declining because of productivity increases, manufacturing will continue to play a role in future U.S. prosperity.

But not if it is disconnected from the "cool cities" research process. Product assembly will probably still drift overseas. But the intersection between research and products — where skilled workers take the research breakthroughs and turn them into products — can remain in the United States. This is the high-value-added part of manufacturing anyway, the part that can afford to pay high wages.

So American cities need to listen to both Florida and Kotkin. And if that means that a factory worker goes to the opera every once in a while, or a scientist goes bowling, that's even better.

2007

The Retirement Factory

Not long ago, I was interviewing a retired politician in a fast-growing Southern metropolis. Even though he was a good old boy who had never left home, he had no resentment for the retired Yankees who flooded his town. In fact, he attributed the whole area's prosperity to them. A retirement community, he said, "is like a high-wage factory. You build 1,000 houses, you have 1,000 households making $90,000 a year. A high-wage factory — without the factory."

I've heard a lot of people make the economic development argument in favor of a retirement-based economy, and it's a hard one to refute. People with money in the bank arrive from somewhere and become part of your community, spending their cash locally and using their knowledge and experience on various do-gooder volunteer tasks. Who wouldn't want that?

But the comparison to a factory got me thinking. A factory is a huge and multi-faceted contribution to a region's economy. Is a retirement community really like a factory?

In some ways the answer to this question is yes — and that's a good thing. The most obvious similarity, as my politician friend pointed out, is that the residents are like factory workers. They live in town, get steady paychecks to spend locally and become involved in local life. Like factory workers, retirees can support a whole service economy with their local spending.

But there's more to a factory-town economy than simply Saturday grocery shopping by the factory workers. That's because factories are in the export business, while retirement communities are in the import business. And an export economy spins off all kinds of economic benefits that you don't get from an import economy. A big factory requires lots of suppliers and tends to stimulate the creation of an entire economic cluster — a group of businesses that can then feed off each other and, in time, find new customers outside the region.

A retirement community creates a cluster of suppliers, too. But these tend to be local service-sector suppliers that create low-wage jobs and aren't interested in repackaging their services for export outside the region — retailers, contractors, landscapers and pool-maintenance companies.

There's also a psychological difference. Factory workers are connected to the local economy in a way that retirees are not. If orders fall off, they might get laid off for a while. They might switch jobs and go to work over at a supplier — sometimes for more money, sometimes for less. But the point is that they have a stake in the regional economy. Factory workers don't like traffic jams anymore than the rest of us, but they see the value of an expanding economy. They see how growth can be good as well as bad.

Retirees see no such thing. They are tied to a global economic system in which their investments are based, or else to the economic fortunes of, say, a government pension system in another part of the country. They might want tax revenue floating into public coffers in New York or Ohio, so their public pension isn't threatened; or they might want interest rates to go up so their income rises.

But they see no benefit in an expanding local economy. If a bunch of factory workers get laid off, the retirees don't need to worry — in fact, they might actually benefit because prices in the local economy might fall. If business is booming and people are employed and labor rates are going up, they don't have to worry about that, either. They might even be harmed by it, because their incomes are fixed — not tied to the local economy — and prices will go up.

Not all retirees view the world in such narrow terms. Many embrace the community to which they move. And retirees can be a wonderful asset because they have time and skills to devote to community causes. But the downsides are typical of any economy based on imports rather than exports, especially the importation of people, whether retirees, part-time residents or tourists.

These economic sectors are only going to grow in the decades ahead, and they do bring significant benefit to many communities. How many formerly rural towns now have a full-time supermarket and drugstore just because of the retirees? But a retirement community brings with it a particular type of economy, one that is not always good for the region hosting it and for many of the regular folk who are trying to make a living because retirement isn't their profession.

2007

Building

The Not-So-Boring Basics

The laptop computer I am writing this column on is plugged into the wall socket in our daughter's bedroom. She is playing the soundtrack from "Boys on the Side" on her CD player. The overhead light is on so everybody can see while I write and my wife helps our daughter pack for winter camp.

This is all a pretty ordinary American scene, with one exception: We live in California — once the land of limitless potential, now the land of rolling blackouts. And no longer do we take it for granted that Sara's songs will play when the CD player is switched on, or that Dad's words will flow when the laptop is plugged in. This is Phase 3 — the most brutal phase so far — in our understanding of how the New Economy works.

Phase 1 came when we realized that computers and the Internet could create whole new business empires — the Microsofts and the Intels, 21st-century equivalents to the New York Central and Southern Pacific .

Phase 2 came when we realized that the real power of the New Economy was to transform the Old Economy — so that manufacturing, shipping, and other boring, old-fashioned things became fast-growing and exciting again.

But in Phase 3, the cold, hard truth has set in. It's not just that the New Economy can transform the Old Economy. The New Economy is dependent on the Old Economy and, in particular, on the boring old "hard" infrastructure that we long ago stopped worrying about because it seemed too expensive, too cumbersome and too environmentally destructive. Like power plants.

Even a decade ago, the conventional wisdom was that the future growth in our nation's power requirements was flat. Now, however, the estimate is that it takes 1 pound of coal to process 2 megabytes of data. That means it will take about one ounce of coal for me to write this column, store it in my computer and transmit it across the country to Governing's office in Washington, D.C. That may not seem like much, but — kind of like traffic — it adds up quickly to a major increase in the demand for new generating capacity, and, indirectly, for more airport capacity, more road capacity, more processing and shipping facilities, and lots of other big-time bricks-and-mortar items.

Nowhere is this more obvious than here in California, where for 20 years we have managed to defy the basic law of economic gravity by growing rich without investing in our basic infrastructure. Ever since Jerry Brown declared an "era of limits" almost a quarter-century ago — and equity-rich NIMBYs began opposing all kinds of things — we have resisted the expansion of virtually everything. Our roads are crowded .

Our airports are so inadequate that a few clouds in the San Francisco sky can confound air travel in the entire Western United States. Our college campuses are exploding with the legacy of a population that has doubled since Ronald Reagan was elected governor. We live in constant fear of a drought. And we are dependent on the kindness of outsiders such as Gary Locke, the governor of Washington, who was able to keep the lights on in California by lending us power.

California is unlikely to build more dams or freeways or airports soon, but we do seem to have a handle on the electricity crisis .

Despite our strict environmental laws and a plant-siting process controlled by a state commission rather than local governments, more than a dozen power plants are under construction. Mostly, they're natural gas-powered plants being constructed near Bakersfield, an oil-producing town that often seems more like Texas than California.

Even for those of us who live on the Left Coast — in an environmentally oriented Democratic state that went solidly for Gore in the last election — there's a lesson here about the basis of our own comfortable prosperity. Without the basics, we're sunk. And that means that the fundamentals of good economic development in the era of the New Economy are a little trickier than we thought.

It's not enough to have a few landscaped business parks where you can park credit-card processors, or even some funky urban neighborhoods where those dot-com "content providers" can commute via Razor scooter.

These economic development success stories — and others as well — are far more dependent than we thought on the basic accoutrements of urban life: airports, highways, power plants, water lines, sewage treatment plants and all the rest of it.

A century ago, the modern metropolis bloomed when the engineers of urban life figured out how to create big, centralized public works systems that move people, electricity, water, waste, goods and all the rest of it. Today, plain ol' infrastructure is still one of the keys to economic development success.

Tax breaks are great and quality of life is important, but no executives are going to be very interested in you if the lights don't come on when they flick the switch and water doesn't come out of the faucet when you turn on the tap.

2001

Paying The Hotel Bill

I don't think anybody in the country has benefited more from public subsidies for convention hotels than I have. I'm a conference rat — often lurking around the hotel and convention center from early in the morning to late at night in search of one more tip, one more trend, one more good yarn about what's going on. It's how I stay in touch.

I wouldn't be able to do this if America's big cities didn't subsidize convention centers and the towering hotels adjacent to them. So maybe I'm not the best person to raise the question of whether such subsidies are a good idea. I guess I should just say, "Thanks, taxpayers."

Actually, the latest question on this front isn't whether subsidies are a good idea. They're probably inevitable. Rather, it's what to do when subsidies aren't enough — when private investors won't build a hotel even when the city is willing to write a big check.

Increasingly, cities and development authorities are building and owning the hotels themselves. This has already happened in Chicago, where the Metropolitan Pier and Exposition Authority floated $108 million in tax-exempt bonds to build and own the Hyatt Regency McCormick Place. It's being discussed in Los Angeles, where civic leaders believe that only a public or nonprofit entity will be willing to build a hotel adjacent to the odd combination of the successful Staples Center and the unsuccessful Los Angeles Convention Center.

A recent analysis of 21 convention hotels by C.H. Johnson Consulting Inc. found that almost half of the development money came from the public sector. In five cities — Chicago, Houston, Austin, Sacramento and Overland Park, Kansas — the public sector paid for 100 percent of the cost of the hotel.

Cities do it because of the paradoxes of the convention business. A successful convention center can attract hundreds of thousands of tourists and hundreds of millions of dollars each year. To succeed, however, the centers need a huge array of ancillary facilities, including hotels, restaurants and retail shops, which can serve as vehicles for extracting tax money from convention-goers' wallets.

But successful convention centers are also behemoths. Although they're often located in or near downtowns, they're so huge that they tend to be separate from everything else that's going on. It's hard for them to feed off the existing infrastructure — and market — for hotels, restaurants and so forth. (This is the problem in Los Angeles, where the convention center is downtown but just far enough away from the hotels to be inconvenient.)

So that's the dilemma. Convention centers need hotels to thrive, but convention hotels are totally hostage to convention-goers. If there's a convention in town, they do fine; otherwise they're empty. So private investors won't touch them — meaning that it's up to the public sector to build the hotel as a piece of infrastructure, kind of like highway off-ramps and parking garages.

But does this make sense? Convention centers can be big winners for cities — garnering publicity, stimulating activity and generating a lot of spinoff sales- and bed-tax revenue. But at some point you have to wonder why it makes sense to go after bed tax and sales tax if you have to pay for and own a $200 million hotel to get it? Or if you have to dedicate all the bed- and sales-tax revenue to paying back the bonds you floated to build the hotel in the first place? In other words, why try to stimulate an economic activity that requires a huge, expensive and completely separate set of infrastructure?

If you look at the most popular convention cities, they fall into two categories: big and cool. The first category involves the places where the convention facilities are so enormous that the biggest conventions have no choice but to go there — such as Las Vegas, Anaheim and Orlando. The problem is, these cities are engaged in a kind of arms race to build ever-bigger facilities. Not everybody can afford to play this game, and most cities that try will lose.

The second category involves the places that have other fun stuff to enjoy besides just the convention center and the hotel — such as San Francisco, New Orleans, Boston, San Diego and Seattle. These are places where the city itself becomes part of the convention attraction, and so the convention infrastructure and the rest of the city feed off one another. This kind of synergy means you don't have to rely on a whole separate convention infrastructure that might lose money. The hotels near San Francisco's Moscone Center are not empty when there is no convention in town.

I know: Not every city can be New Orleans or Boston, just as not every city can afford the Anaheim-Las Vegas arms race. But I'm naive enough to believe that every city is special, and building "cool" is more feasible than building "big." On the other hand, maybe I'm just tired of hanging around convention hotels surrounded by nothing but parking garages and freeway off-ramps.

2002

Why The Shovels Matter

Many billions of dollars are now flowing from Washington to the states and cities in the hopes that they will help to create jobs and rekindle national prosperity. The money is going for all kinds of things, from "shovel ready" road-building and repair projects to augmented social services benefits to funds for energy conservation efforts. But there's little question that the Holy Grail of this effort is jobs — lots of them, turning up really soon, putting money in people's pockets and pulling the country out of the deep economic downturn that has now lasted the better part of two years.

There's a relevant question to ask here, and I wouldn't be surprised if you were asking it right now. Don't the states have big economic development programs in place already? Aren't the states "laboratories of democracy," creative sources of entrepreneurship where innovative ideas about economic policies are often test-driven? Wouldn't it make sense for all this state-level economic development to become the first line of attack deployed in the service of national economic recovery?

Well, not necessarily. The reason is that economic recovery and economic development are two entirely different things. The first one is a short-term effort to kick-start the economy when conditions turn bad. The second is a long-term effort to create enduring prosperity through a whole variety of means, such as recruiting new businesses to your state and helping to grow them at home. States — and local governments, too — are frequently good at economic development, especially if they are able to approach it strategically and consistently over a long period of time. But even the biggest states — and obviously the biggest municipalities as well — are not well positioned to influence short-term economic recovery.

The reason is that they just don't have the right tools for the effort. In down times, states and municipalities may possess ingenuity, know-how, economic development savvy — all kinds of advantages. But there are a couple of valuable cards they can't play. Obviously, they don't have the ability to influence the national or global economic forces that are causing the downturn in the first place. And second, in a down economy, they don't have the one commodity required above all others to kick-start the process — substantial amounts of money.

Even though they lack the breadth to deal with large-scale economic problems, state and local governments sometimes try to use the tools they do have to make a dent. As I reported in a column a few months ago, it's relatively common for local governments to waive fees for developers in hopes of getting the local real estate market going. Since I wrote that, some California cities have taken this one step further, offering to foot the sales tax bill for local residents buying cars from local auto dealers. In many cases, this is a drastic move to help the dealers — who may be on the verge of going under.

Such measures may help to ameliorate the situation a little, but they won't turn things around. These days, a recession isn't local or even regional. It's national or global. And that's the reason why it usually requires federal action to stimulate the economy.

And the feds can borrow — or, if necessary, print — money on a large scale. Unlike the federal government, states and localities are usually required by their constitution or their charter to balance their budgets. They can't deficit-spend their way out of a recession on a program of Keynesian economics. They can sometimes engage in financial tricks through which long-term bond funds can be used, essentially, to pay current bills, as New York famously did back in the

'70s and as California has been doing to a lesser extent to get out of short-term budget trouble in more recent years.

But these tricks are not usually undertaken in the service of economic recovery; in most cases, a state or city resorts to this chicanery to balance the budget and avoid facing painful political reality. That can provide a weird and temporary kind of economic stability — people aren't thrown out of work, at least not right away — but it's no strategy for climbing out of an economic hole and staying out.

So what can states — and localities — do, other than just grab the money coming out of Washington as quickly as possible? After all, there's not much time for strategic thinking when the federal government says you have to spend the stimulus money within 120 days.

Maybe the answer really is to be "shovel ready." The state and local governments that are going to benefit from the stimulus package the most — the ones that will get the most bang for the buck and move their economies back to prosperity most quickly — are those that did their strategic thinking long ago. They didn't wait for the stimulus package to start mulling what their priorities should be and which projects to pursue. They'd already identified their biggest needs — and now they can use the stimulus money to make some of those things happen.

And that's ultimately what economic development is all about: setting the table, planning ahead, understanding how to spend the next dollar, the next grant, the next infusion of stimulus money to its greatest effect. In this recession, the best economic development effort is the one that was completed before the recession began.

2009

Locating

Keeping The Feds Downtown

It's not hard to understand why the FBI office in New Haven, Connecticut, wants to relocate. The Robert N. Giaimo Federal Building isn't that old, dating from the 1960s, but it is literally falling apart. When it rains, agent Merrill Parks told a recent news conference, "it looks like Yosemite Falls in my office."

The question is where the FBI will go. The U.S. General Services Administration, which handles most federal real estate matters, has cast a wide net, looking at 27 buildings in the New Haven area. Sixteen are in the suburbs, and that hasn't gone down too well with officials at City Hall. In fact, it wasn't long before city officials showed up at the GSA, waving an 18-year-old executive order from President Jimmy Carter requiring federal agencies to weigh the impact of their actions on America's downtowns.

Now both the GSA and the FBI say they're committed to New Haven, and they're working with city officials to try to find a downtown location. But the New Haven case, along with several others nationwide, has highlighted the role federal offices play in shaping downtowns and other business districts.

The federal government is in the midst of one of the biggest building booms ever. Just one example: Currently, more than 30 federal courthouses are under construction at a cost of over $2 billion, and

156 more are pending before Congress. And that's just the judiciary. Furthermore, GSA has recently made a renewed commitment to architectural quality, imposing stricter guidelines and hiring big- name architects.

Even as all this is going on, however, downtown advocates say the federal government has been rapidly suburbanizing federal jobs. Now they're leaning on the Clinton administration to reverse the tide. The Council on Urban Economic Development and the International Downtown Association are negotiating with GSA to come up with a new version of the Carter executive order that will revise siting and building standards to give downtowns a leg up for federal offices.

When downtowns had to reinvent themselves as big retailers withdrew in the '50s and '60s, government offices usually formed the foundation of the "new downtowns" — providing tenants for office buildings, shoppers for remaining retailers and patrons for public transit. In some states, such as California, the state government has had an explicit policy of reinforcing downtowns. In other states, the policy has been implicit but vital — as with New York State's extensive leasing in the Empire State Building and the World Trade Center.

But the real estate boom touched off by Reagan-era tax cuts (and subsequently shut down by Reagan-era tax reform) encouraged office construction in the suburbs, putting pressure on GSA to lease space there. And that, in turn, is what led the downtown lobby to resurrect the Carter executive order. In particular, the downtowners have pointed to several cases — including New Haven — where GSA has proposed moving federal offices out of federally designated "empowerment communities" — special zones where local governments receive federal assistance to stimulate job growth.

In some cases, suburban locations may offer lower rents and shorter commutes for some federal workers and federal agency "customers." But downtown advocates rightly argue that downtowns still hold certain advantages. They are centrally located and accessible by public transit — a big advantage for an agency such as the Social Security Administration. And in today's sprawling metropolises, there's often more than one downtown in a region — as in the New York area, with Manhattan, downtown Brooklyn and Newark — so options aren't always limited.

But there is one more reason for a renewed government commitment to downtowns, and that's money. Many downtowns are reinventing themselves yet again because of business downsizing. The big corporations and professional firms that have fueled downtown growth in the past 20 years are cutting back or disappearing altogether. And that means many gleaming skyscrapers (some built with federal assistance, such as the old Urban Development Action Grant program) are emptying out.

Real estate experts say they expect government offices to form the foundation for yet another "new" era in downtowns by leasing up space at cheap prices. In Los Angeles, the local school district has moved some offices into elegantly appointed downtown space. The district's a little embarrassed about the plush space — but not about the price, which is cheaper even than office space in outlying districts.

Having thrown subsidies at downtowns for a half-century in hopes of propping them up, there's no reason the federal government shouldn't reaffirm its commitment to leasing downtown space — and reap the financial benefits of a soft market in the process.

1996

Is Competition Worth The Price?

Anybody who has ever bought breakfast cereal knows that a market-oriented society means individuals have to make more choices. Where there used to be five cereals, now there are 70. Where there used to be one telephone company, now there are 20. To the average person, this expansion of choice is usually either liberating or bewildering — or sometimes both.

What is often overlooked, however, is the fact that the headlong rush to a market-oriented society also means whole communities must make choices as well. Local governments are increasingly thrown into their own bewildering world of multiplying options. Faced with the need to cut costs in order to stay competitive, they are rapidly disconnecting themselves from traditional economic relationships in ways that would have been simply impossible a generation ago.

Take, for example, the small town of Bristol, a community of 20,000 people in southern Virginia just across the border from its "twin city" of Bristol, Tennessee. In an unprecedented act, Bristol recently unplugged itself from the federal Tennessee Valley Authority, the largest power company in the United States, and started buying power from Cinergy Co. of Cincinnati, which promised a $70 million cut in the town's electricity prices over 10 years. As one local official said, $70 million can buy you a lot of freedom to pursue economic development projects in a small town.

This is a big change. For most of the recent past, large segments of every local economy have been protected from competition — the telephone company, the electric utility, the cable TV provider, the hospital, the bus and airline companies that served the town. Some of these arrangements, like the TVA, were left over from the Depression and earlier populist periods in American history, when whole industries were essentially removed from the marketplace for the apparent well-being of society. In a period when pressure to cut costs was low, these protected businesses provided a stable bedrock on which to build the rest of the local economy.

But almost all of them now face competition in the local marketplace, with electric utilities the last to be deregulated. Both public and private power companies have long operated in a highly regulated environment that removed choice from the hands of individuals and communities as the price of stability. Now economic pressures are forcing change. California and several other states have already passed sweeping deregulation bills, and Congress is likely to endorse the movement toward choice with legislation of its own.

Many public officials — state, local and federal — embrace this wholesale change as a way to "level the playing field" and make their communities more competitive. Republican U.S. Representative Bob Franks of New Jersey, for example, wants to use utility deregulation to end what he views as regional inequities in power rates.

Franks' complaint with the current system is that Northeastern utility rates are considerably higher than rates in the South and the West, where much of the electricity is provided by federal power companies such as TVA or Bonneville Power Administration. To Franks, the presence of these federal entities — designed to promote economic development in their own regions, which historically needed the help — has created an unfair situation that puts his own state at a disadvantage.

"We use New Jersey federal tax dollars to subsidize somebody from the TVA to fly up to New Jersey and take away my jobs," he recently told a meeting of the National Council on Urban Economic

Development. (For its part, the TVA claims it is self-supporting.) As Congress approaches the task of deregulating electric utilities, Franks views his task in economic development terms. He wants to use deregulation to eliminate whatever advantage the federal power companies might give to the South and West.

Of course, electric utilities — along with hospitals, phone companies, and other traditionally protected economic actors — have themselves played an important role in promoting local economies. They couldn't afford not to: They didn't want their huge capital investments "stranded" in geographical areas that were in decline. But now that attitude is, inevitably, changing. Instead of being wedded to specific geographical areas, utilities, phone companies, hospitals and all the rest are becoming more footloose, chasing profits wherever they can be found — just as manufacturing companies have been doing for decades.

Whether or not the change to utility competition is a good idea, it's probably inevitable, given the tumultuous, market-oriented world we live in. In Bristol, the big question is not whether unplugging from the TVA is smart, but whether $70 million is enough to make up for the loss of stability. There, and everywhere else in the country, we'll have to wait and see whether competition is worth the price we pay for it.

1997

Downtown Digs For The Placeless Office

I could work anywhere. Or, at least, that's what everybody tells me. As a researcher, writer and urban planner, my job is the kind that seems to require little more than a PC, a modem and a telephone. So I should be able to work on a mountaintop, or along a babbling brook, or in some other beautiful and isolated place that will constantly renew and restore me. Right?

Wrong. Although I worked at home for many years, now I work in a small office in a small downtown area in the city where I live. Instead of a mountaintop, I have a view of a crumbling Art Deco movie theater. Instead of a babbling brook, I often hear babbling transients loitering on the street outside.

So why do I do it? Because I need it. In this office, I have easy access to other writers and planners located nearby. The post office is across the street. It's 20 steps to the FedEx box. In contrast to the mountaintop, I'm in the middle of everything I need to be in touch with.

And I am not the only one who feels those needs. In a new paper entitled "Linking the New Economy to the Livable Community," a group of researchers at Collaborative Economics, a Silicon Valley-based firm, has put forth a seemingly revolutionary notion: Rather than further isolating us on mountaintops and in sprawling subdivisions, as is often predicted, the digital economy will actually push us closer together into downtowns and other compact work environments. That's where the companies and the workers who are driving this "new economy" will want to be, and that's where the small-scale, latte-drinking ethos of these businesses will most likely flourish.

"At each stage in our country's economic evolution," authors Doug Henton and Kim Walesh report, "economic change has led to a fundamental reconfiguration of the places where we live and work." By focusing on knowledge, speed and flexibility, they say the "new" economy is decentralizing workplaces and companies, creating more mobile workers and causing a new emphasis on geographical clustering and quality of life. The result, in their view, is that the "new" economy will increasingly prove compatible with the urban design philosophy of the "new urbanism," with its emphasis on compact, dense development and pedestrian-oriented neighborhoods.

This is not what the experts predicted in the 1980s. At the dawn of the PC age, the assumption was that by eliminating the need for big workplaces, the digital economy would simply accelerate the physical decentralization of our economy and of our society. If you don't need to be in midtown Manhattan, why not be off by yourself on a beach somewhere?

A decade later, some people have moved to the beach or the wilderness. But most people haven't. The PC and the modem may have freed us from an old-fashioned commute to a big downtown. But they have not severed the umbilical cord to the metropolitan economy, nor have they eliminated the need for "face time."

So most of us live and work in what might be called "the suburban workshop" — commuting not to big downtown offices but to "Edge Cities" somewhere fairly close to home that still allow us access to other people and other businesses when we need them. As the Community Economics report points out, in a freelance-style world where small businesses have to pick up new teams of workers for virtually every project, the "transaction cost" of searching all over the country for recruits can be very high. Geographical clustering and easy access to a whole metropolitan area can bring those costs down.

Does this necessarily mean that the "new economy" translates into the "new urbanism"? In some cases, clearly the answer is yes. The software and "new media" businesses are a good example. Software companies have begun to cluster in the traditionally 9-to-5 environment of downtown San Jose, especially since the city persuaded Adobe to move into a downtown high-rise by billing it as a "vertical campus." The new media hipsters, meanwhile, have clustered in a Soho-style urban neighborhood in San Francisco, rather than in the more suburban environment of the Silicon Valley.

But is this true of the rest of us? Does a five-minute walk really make for a lower transaction cost than a five-minute drive? That's a more debatable point. Even if they work in smaller units closer to home, most people still live in suburbs — and most of those suburbs are autobound. To travel from my home to my new office, I have little choice but to drive. The downtown location is more expensive than offices closer to my home. And I had to make the difficult decision to locate myself farther away from my daughter's school during the workday. A lot of other new-economy dads might have made a different choice. The new economy may be a good fit with the new urbanism, but it doesn't always make the old suburb obsolete.

1998

Living The Niche Life

After 16 years of suburbia, I now live in a downtown. Ventura's downtown is not big — only a dozen or so blocks end to end. But it's a downtown most American cities would kill to have, with a historic fabric, movies and live theater, dozens of restaurants and lots of retail stores.

Since I moved, I've become more of an urbanite — eating out more often, running more errands without using my car. My teenage daughter is quickly making a way of life out of walks to Starbucks, jogging down Main Street and taking the bus everywhere instead of being chauffeured by me.

And I am not alone. Plenty of other people live in or near my downtown, and, motivated by high California home prices, developers have teed up 800 new housing units to be constructed here in the near future. In my town, as elsewhere in the country, living downtown seems to be the latest trend.

Wistful urban planners claim that this is simply a return to the way things used to be — a time when everybody lived "above the store" in close proximity to jobs and everyday services. In fact, however, such nostalgia isn't quite accurate. As MIT professor Robert Fogelson points out in his excellent recent book Downtown, the emergence of the American downtown between 1880 and 1920 was based on the opposite premise: that a downtown was exclusively a business district where nobody lived.

In fact, Fogelson argues, the American downtown — especially in large cities — was actually part of the engine that fueled suburban growth during the streetcar and early automobile eras. In those days, civic promoters believed that cities had a kind of inherent duality: Businesses were centralized in downtown, while residents were dispersed in suburban districts. Indeed, many urban leaders argued that these two forces worked together, that as a downtown became more and more densely developed with office and retail uses, this permitted the residential population to become more and more dispersed in the outer residential areas that were being created at the time.

As early as the late 1920s — and certainly after World War II — this theory was proven wrong. It was inevitable that retail and office businesses would follow their customers and their workforce out of downtowns and into outlying areas. This created a crisis among real estate investors who had staked so much on the downtowns. These investors, Fogelson argues, actually appropriated the ideas of urban renewal and "slum clearance" from housing advocates as a way of boosting downtown fortunes.

But one thing is clear in Fogelson's history: During downtown's heyday, nobody actually lived there. There may have been flophouses and declining working-class districts on the outskirts, but in order to gather the vast number of people required as workers and shoppers, downtowns depended not on local housing but on modern transportation systems, especially trolleys.

So when people talk these days about creating a vibrant downtown by building housing, they are not talking about the way things used to be. They are talking about a revolution — inserting housing into districts that, historically, were used exclusively for offices and stores.

This revolution is not likely to counteract the ongoing march of suburbia. Nationwide, the downtown housing numbers are tiny — a few thousand units here and there, compared with millions in outlying areas. But there is a downtown housing movement for several reasons.

One of the most important is that downtowns themselves have changed. Rather than serving as the one-stop shop for practically all retail and office-based businesses in a city, they have emerged as a kind of lifestyle alternative. General retail and office uses have been on the wane in downtowns for many years, and they have been replaced by entertainment-oriented retail such as theaters and restaurants.

Some people like living in close proximity to these amenities, and they're willing to make tradeoffs that most people are unwilling to make — less living space, higher housing costs, more traffic noise, tough parking situations. Far from being a place where everybody goes, downtowns are becoming a niche market where a few people live. Indeed, one of my concerns about downtown Ventura is that it will simply become an entertainment-oriented bedroom suburb for pricey Santa Barbara, 30 miles up the road.

Some things aren't any more convenient downtown than they are anywhere else. I still have to schlep my car to the supermarket and the big-box retailers just as I always did. And urban living has its downside, too. The police visit my block every once in a while, and the homeless wander by on a regular basis.

But I can walk to my local farmers' market, and the 10-screen movie theater is just past the library. And even though I get skittish about giving my daughter more freedom, I always know she's somewhere in the neighborhood. I'll take the trade.

2004

The Home Equity Divide

In July 2005, at the absolute peak of the real estate boom here in Southern California, I did what lots of other people were doing: I bought a house for a very expensive price with an adjustable rate mortgage. The price was far more than I ever imagined I'd pay — probably triple what the same property would have cost in, say, 1998.

Before long, interest rates started creeping upward and home prices flattened out. Soon, I was paying more in mortgage. Yet if I had to sell, I'd probably get less than I paid. All of which means I'm stuck making high payments on a very expensive house. I have to make a very good income to keep doing this but moving would make it worse.

Across the country in Upstate New York, a friend of mine recently lost his job. He thought about moving back to Long Island where he grew up, but he quickly realized he was on the other side of the home-equity divide from me. His house was worth about half of what I had put down on my house. Moving back to Long Island would mean paying four or five times the value of his current home for a new house. He was stuck, too — in a very cheap house, without a job.

The ebb and flow of the housing market determines a lot about the economic viability of regions. It is an article of faith among economists that for a region to prosper, the housing market must be in equilibrium. A large supply of housing must be available at a variety of price points to accommodate the local population and especially those who work in the community.

Yet, increasingly, this isn't what is going on. The fabled "Big Sort" — the sorting out of America's metropolitan areas into winners and losers — has birthed a new phenomenon: the "Big Stuckness." People who ought to be more mobile are stuck.

In "hot" regions — especially on the coasts — housing markets can easily become overheated. But when they cool down, the base price is much higher than ever before, creating a kind of permanent unaffordability. In "cold" regions, especially in the interior of the nation, the housing market never gains any momentum, and thus local residents never accumulate much equity.

Sometimes, of course, the fact that people are stuck in a house — and the way they're stuck — can benefit the local economy. Here in Southern California, millions of people can afford to work at middle-class jobs because they bought their houses for a fraction of what they would cost today. So they sit on their expensive homes and stay in the local workforce even though, based on their incomes, they can't afford to live in the region.

In Upstate New York, hundreds of thousands of people — maybe millions — are content in their inexpensive homes. They're reluctant to move, even though economic theory would suggest they should.

Overall, though, the benefits of the Big Stuckness are temporary. In my town, the teachers, police officers and nurses sitting on $800,000 houses are gradually selling out to people who can pay the sticker price — affluent retirees or commuters to nearby towns where wages are higher. The people taking their place in the job market can't live here. Truthfully, I'm not sure where they'll live.

And in regions like Upstate New York, the downside of living in a depressed economy usually outweighs the upside of affordable housing, especially for young people looking for opportunity. Because the young don't own houses, they're mobile. It's their aging parents who are stuck.

You'd think that the disparate economics of home ownership around the nation would create a kind of equilibrium. Sooner or later, it would seem as though California and Boston and Washington, D.C., would become too expensive, and so business activity would drift inland to the other side of the Big Sort.

Surprisingly, however, this doesn't seem to be the case. Some jobs do leave New York for Scranton, or Los Angeles for Montana, but they're such footloose jobs that soon they are in Ireland or India. Meanwhile, the real economic engines in the winning regions pretty much stay put no matter how high home prices go. For those who drive the economy, the benefits of being in a winning region are so great that the cost of housing becomes secondary.

In the meantime, a lot of us are stuck right now — in a house so expensive we can barely afford to stay or a house so cheap we can't afford to leave.

2007

Creating

Who's Competitive In The New Economy?

It's hard to imagine two metropolitan areas more different than Los Angeles and Rochester, New York. One is in the West, the other in the East. One is big, the other small. One is sunny, the other snowy. One is growing, the other shrinking. One, in the popular image, is hip to the New Economy. The other is not.

Yet according to a new study ranking American metropolitan areas by their potential for New Economy growth, Los Angeles and Rochester are almost exactly alike. They rank 20th and 21st out of 50 major metro areas in their New Economy potential, and their scores on the Progressive Policy Institute's "Metropolitan New Economy Index" equal the national average almost exactly.

How can two cities be alike when they're so different? It turns out that when it comes to the New Economy, no metropolitan area is without assets. And no metropolitan area has a monopoly on success. Well, maybe some do. At the top of PPI's index are a few familiar names: San Francisco, Austin, Seattle, Raleigh-Durham, San Diego, Washington and Boston. These are the hands-down winners in the New Economy competition so far. But as venture capitalists look beyond the obvious locations for the new opportunities, the next round of winners isn't so obvious.

PPI's index used 16 different indicators to assemble the rankings, including "gazelles" (fast-growing companies), publicly traded companies, high-tech jobs and patents issued. San Francisco — no surprise here — was in a class by itself. Austin was a distant but strong second, and the other top locations were clumped together farther back.

Once you get down to the "average" places, each city has assets and liabilities, and the combination of the two is always different, which suggests that each metro area should pursue a different economic development strategy.

It's not surprising, for example, that L.A. outclasses Rochester in a wide range of categories. L.A. ranked 12th in "gazelle" companies, while Rochester ranked only 40th. L.A. took 9th place in online population (40 percent of the population using computers) whereas Rochester was dead last, with only 25 percent. L.A. ranked second in the number of registered commercial Internet domains, whereas Rochester ranked 28th.

Their overall ranking was almost exactly the same because Rochester has a lot of assets that L.A. doesn't have. A longtime corporate town- -home to both Xerox and Kodak — Rochester has a strong managerial class (ranking 31st in managerial and professional jobs compared with 42nd for L.A.). It ranks fifth in computer use in the schools, whereas L.A ranks 47th.

Thanks to the Rochester Institute of Technology and other local schools, Rochester ranks sixth in science-engineering and 11th in academic research and development funding, where L.A. was 30th in each. Between the universities and corporations, Rochester ranked first in patents issued (L.A. was 28th). Indeed, Rochester's ratio of 2.33 patents per 1,000 workers was more than 50 percent higher than the ratio in San Francisco and Austin, which ranked second and third, respectively, in that category. When you break down the New Economy this way, it becomes pretty clear why both Los Angeles and Rochester are "average." L.A. has a huge and technologically hip population, as well as a lot of business activity. But it's also an immigrant town, which makes work-force training and education a huge challenge that the region can't seem to overcome.

Rochester, on the other hand, has an extraordinary base of economic infrastructure capable of supporting the New Economy, including a long history of tech-oriented companies, great universities and a work force capable of bringing innovation into the marketplace. What drags Rochester down is not an Old Economy reality, but something resembling an Old Economy attitude. Nobody's hanging around on the Internet at home, and it's apparently a tough climate for tech start-ups.

So, while L.A. has the money and the entrepreneurial zeal, the region's challenge is to bring a huge population of recent immigrants along for the ride. For Rochester, it's mostly the opposite problem — the workers and the ideas are there, but the region's economic leaders have to bust out of the 1960s, encourage tech-smart kids to stay in Rochester and help them get started.

I've lived half my life just outside Rochester and the other half just outside Los Angeles. At first glance, I, like most people, would lay my money on L.A. as a New Economy winner. Yet after looking at the Metropolitan New Economy Index, I'm not so sure. Bringing a sense of upward mobility and high-tech entrepreneurship to millions of recent immigrants is a daunting task. Changing the attitudes of a few bankers and civic leaders — or replacing them — seems simpler by comparison. And that's why there's no guarantee that places such as L.A. will be New Economy winners and places such as Rochester will be New Economy losers. A decade from now, it could just as easily be the other way around.

2001

The Spawning Spark

Lately I've been going around telling people that I'm an entrepreneur. Five years ago, I moved my freelance business out of the house, opened an office and began looking for a secretary. Today, the resulting company has seven employees including myself. This doesn't exactly qualify me for the Silicon Valley or Route 128 Hall of Fame, but I am proud of it. Somehow or other I've created something out of nothing.

As a startup business owner, I never really thought about how or why I became an entrepreneur — or, in the lingo of some folks who study entrepreneurship, how I was spawned in this regard. For me, it was pretty simple. I was busting out of the house, I needed staff help, and as the economy boomed it looked like my business was going to keep growing.

But it turns out that I was not a typical entrepreneur at all. I had spent most of my professional life flying solo as a freelancer. For most entrepreneurs, the spawning process begins at a big company, where skills are learned, contacts are made and the gumption is found to go out on one's own.

Understanding this spawning process is vitally important to economic development: Entrepreneurs still drive a lot of the innovative opportunities in our economy. A new report from the Global Entrepreneurship Monitor, a joint effort of Babson College, the London Business School and the Kauffman Foundation, found that about 10 percent of American workers are employed by entrepreneurial startups less than four years old. That's down from 16 percent in the Internet bubble days of three years ago, but it's still a considerable chunk. Just as important — especially from an economic development perspective — is that, despite all the publicity, entrepreneurial activity is not focused in Silicon Valley and Route 128. It's spread pretty evenly across the nation, for the simple reason that entrepreneurs come in all shapes and sizes and businesses, not just in technology.

This is good news for states and localities outside the high-tech mainstream, which often view themselves as being left behind in the entrepreneurial economy. But there is more to entrepreneurship than these raw numbers, and this makes leveraging business ventures through public policy more difficult. First, true entrepreneurship — as most of us have learned the hard way — requires venture capital, and venture capital is still extremely concentrated in one economic sector (high tech) and two geographical locations (Massachusetts' Route 128 and California's Silicon Valley). And second, the spawning of entrepreneurs requires talented folks sitting at a big company thinking about going off on their own.

But what kinds of folks, and in what kind of big company? This was the subject of a second recent study, this one by Paul Gompers and Josh Lerner of the Harvard Business School and David Scharfstein at MIT's Sloan School. In examining what they call "entrepreneurial spawning," the three authors found — somewhat to their surprise — that entrepreneurs are not smart business executives who are fed up with the bloated and bureaucratic ways of their employer. Rather, they are people who work for companies that have themselves been started by entrepreneurs. In other words, entrepreneurs are spawned by the excitement of working in an entrepreneurial environment.

Of course, the Harvard-MIT study dealt only with venture capital- backed startups, which means it might be too skewed toward the Silicon Valley/Route 128 types. And therein lies one of the difficulties that economic developers face in dealing with startup companies: The rich seem to get richer. Venture capitalists make money off of high-tech startups and therefore seek to recirculate money in places such as Silicon Valley, where budding entrepreneurs can see that their current bosses have gotten rich off the process. Meanwhile, the rest of the country suffers from a lack of venture capital investment, and so would-be entrepreneurs stare at the ceiling while working for stodgy corporations.

At least that's how it seems looking at the data. But there may be a number of ways around this problem for state and local officials. First, many communities have begun to create their own venture capital funds — sometimes with public subsidies but more often by persuading local investors to put their venture capital to work locally rather than in Silicon Valley. Second, a few entrepreneurs are willing to leave Silicon Valley to set up shop in their hometowns, using venture capital startup funds to do so. Doug Burgum of Great Plains Software, located in Fargo, North Dakota, is a great example. And third, communities around the nation can benefit from entrepreneur-driven expansion even if they don't have the entrepreneurs or venture capital locally, simply by understanding how to provide goods and services to the high-growth sectors of the economy.

So the situation for most communities may not be as bleak as it first appears. Of course, localities around the country should also honor and recognize those small entrepreneurs who make an important contribution as well — even if it's only seven jobs. I'm still waiting for my Entrepreneur of the Year Award.

2003

Opening Up The Innovation Process

Seventy-five years ago, at the dawn of the Great Depression, the owners of the Columbian Rope Co. made a daring move. While other manufacturing companies were cutting back, Columbian pressed forward with plans to create a "New Products Research Laboratory" adjacent to the rope company's large factory in upstate New York.

The young scientist Columbian selected to run the lab was my grandfather, Edgar Johnson, then a chemistry professor at Cornell University. It was a classic example of private industry luring a significant talent out of academia. In 1930, Johnson left the cozy intellectual sophistication of Ithaca and moved his family — including my concert-pianist grandmother — forty miles north to the factory town of Auburn.

The gamble paid off. By the late 1930s, Columbian was producing innovative breakthroughs in rope strength that helped the company dominate the field. During World War II, the research lab tackled "rope rot," experimenting with the first chemical treatments designed to slow down the decay caused by fungi, mold and other organisms. Over the course of three decades, my grandfather's R&D operation helped make Columbian the second-largest rope company in the world, secured Auburn's reputation as "the cordage city" and helped provide the community with good factory jobs — even for people I went to high school with many years later. It was, in other words, one of Auburn's most effective economic development tools.

Columbian's research lab was, of course, a classic corporate R&D operation — a proprietary lab operating in secret, located across the street from the factory and far away from the academic world of chemistry. Today the story would be different. Edgar Johnson might be lured away from teaching, but he would probably not be lured far from the Cornell campus — perhaps to a research lab set up by Cornell and funded partly by Columbian. His discoveries would not be proprietary. They would probably be at least partly in the public domain and applied to specific products by a combination of academics, researchers and corporations. The discoveries would be brought to market through joint ventures, partnerships, licensing agreements and similar techniques.

This is the difference between the closed approach to research that was the norm in my grandfather's day and the so-called "open innovation" approach. As outlined in a book by the same name by Harvard professor Henry William Chesbrough, the "open innovation" idea calls for a more public and collaborative approach as a way of developing new products, especially in the technology sector. By placing research labs close to college campuses and sharing knowledge more openly, the idea goes, we are more likely to see successful spinoff companies, and the flow of profitable new products will accelerate.

In addition to turning the traditional corporate research model on its head, the open innovation approach suggests a much greater emphasis on public policy as well. Open innovation must be undertaken by an entire community — not by an individual company. And that means investments and commitment by the public and nonprofit sectors as well as private companies. San Diego became a leader in biotechnology because of a series of public investments in land and other startup efforts for a series of institutions: UC San Diego, Scripps Research Institute, the Salk Institute, which are located in close proximity to one another. More recently, Arizona's leaders have kicked in $90 million to start the Translational Genomics Research Institute (TGEN) and are now creating a medical school in Phoenix with a translational genomics emphasis. Another striking example is California's

Proposition 71, which makes a $6 billion state commitment to stem-cell research, largely to reestablish the state's lead in biotechnology.

Decades ago, Auburn's industrial leaders set the table for economic growth in many ways. There were the rail connections, the power lines and many other pieces of underlying infrastructure that any manufacturing company required. Then there were the early versions of the Richard Florida "creative class" theory. Not the least of Auburn's economic development efforts, I'm sure, was providing opportunities for my grandmother to perform with symphony orchestras, which in turn made life in Auburn more attractive for my grandfather.

But Auburn working together with ivory-tower Ithaca to create research labs that connected academia to the world of manufacturing? Fostering networks among researchers whose employers were in competition for new products and market share? Using "open innovation" to create synergies between people who don't talk to each other? That was ahead of Edgar Johnson's time. It's interesting to wonder how much stronger rope would be today if open innovation had been in vogue decades ago.

2004

Upping The Ante On Stem Cell Research

Here in California, we are often on the cutting edge of economic development. Now we're about to enter a whole new realm, thanks to the recent passage of Proposition 71, the stem-cell initiative.

Although it won almost 60 percent of the votes cast in November — Prop. 71 is one of the most peculiar pieces of public policy you'll ever see. It requires a nearly bankrupt state to float $3 billion in bonds to fund basic medical research of the type that the federal government or private research institutions typically undertake. This money is to be doled out by a board that will be mostly insulated from political oversight. Its members will be individuals, such as representatives of universities and research centers that would certainly be viewed under other state laws as having a conflict of interest. And the measure was enthusiastically supported by a Republican governor, even though this governor had previously opposed all new state debt and also campaigned for an incumbent president who is morally opposed to most of the research agenda.

But what's at stake, in economic development terms, is enormous. And if the Prop. 71 gamble succeeds, it could alter the state-level economic development stakes in a profound way.

State-level economic development efforts usually are focused on jobs. A state might target a sector of the economy that could be lured into the state or is at risk of leaving. Then the state's economic development officials offer to build roads and other infrastructure, train employees, provide tax breaks or sometimes even give cash payments to companies that relocate, stay or expand in the state. The most generous view is that state economic development efforts help build and retain a business and jobs base that is a good match for the state. The most cynical view is that state economic development efforts do nothing more than buy jobs. But one thing is constant: State efforts target companies and jobs that already exist.

Prop. 71 seeks to use state funds — borrowed funds, no less — to stimulate basic medical research that will presumably keep California at the forefront of the biotech economy for the next decade or two. No one disputes that there is boundless economic opportunity in the new treatments and therapies resulting from medical breakthroughs in stem-cell research and related fields. And California — although expensive, crowded and broke as a state government — still has a vast and impressive biotech infrastructure.

By passing Prop. 71, however, California has taken an unprecedented step for a state: It is essentially replacing the federal government as the funder of basic research needed to create biotech breakthroughs. Many regions have used biotech as an economic development engine by developing research institutions that will spin-off breakthroughs, patents and nearby companies. But usually they have done so by competing for federal research dollars, especially from the National Institutes of Health.

In the case of Prop. 71, however, California is exploiting an opening created by President Bush's moral qualms about stem-cell research. Dominated by "Red State" thinking, the federal government is severely constrained in conducting stem-cell research and is unlikely to play its customary role as the funder of basic breakthroughs. By contrast, voters in the Big Blue State have agreed to make stem-cell research a constitutional right under the state constitution. Ironically, Blue States such as California may reap huge economic benefits if they are willing to pursue medical research that Bush and other Red State conservatives are reluctant to support.

California is not alone in trying to kick-start the biotech sector. Arizona raised $90 million for the Phoenix-based Translational Genomics Institute. Florida is contributing hundreds of millions of dollars for the East Coast branch of San Diego-based Scripps Research Institute. But the passage of Prop. 71 is upping the ante more than anybody imagined. Already, research scientists are flowing out of the Washington, D.C., area to California. And Arizona is fearful that the celebrated TGEN effort is pint-sized in comparison.

The exact payoff to California is hard to estimate. No one can predict how much economic activity Prop. 71 will stimulate or how much of the likely bonanza California will be able to retain. The initiative vaguely requires that the state benefit economically from patents and other breakthroughs but doesn't specify how. But there is little question that a payoff will come and that California will retain its lead in the biotech field because of Prop. 71.

The old-fashioned game of chasing jobs probably won't go away. After all, governors love to cut ribbons at factories — even our movie-star governor here in California. But in passing Prop. 71, we in California may be leading the states into a previously uncharted territory. In the future, it won't be enough to target the jobs. States also will have to invest in the breakthroughs.

2005

The New Economy Still Needs Martinizing

The latest big news at the University of Arizona Science and Technology Park in Tucson isn't about patents or genetics or nanotechnology. It's about Martinizing.

Yes, you can now get your dry-cleaning done inside the research park. It's just one example of how university research parks are changing as America's economic engines change.

"The first generation of university research parks were real estate propositions — land and buildings," says Bruce Wright, chief operating officer for the University of Arizona park. They were warehouses for R&D, located close to campus.

Some companies still need the secure campus-like setting that traditional business parks offer. But these companies have to be big in order to justify the canteens and the fitness centers the parks offer. And they have to have a good reason for being insular, such as defense contracts or proprietary products.

Today, such companies are stagnant at best. The Communist-era defense programs have shut down, and the high-tech firms have been shifting engineering and R&D operations overseas.

A few years ago, university research parks moved into a second phase, focusing on facilitating technology transfer and commercialization. This caused a change as to what happened inside the buildings — the activities were smaller scale and more closely aligned with the nearby university — but it didn't change the parks themselves or the way they related to the world around them.

Now there's a third wave. It is one where "university research parks must play in the global economy — partner with other research parks around the world — and help small-and mid-sized tech companies," says Wright, who is one of dozens of university research park specialists around the country attempting to capitalize on this wave.

Smaller still than their predecessors and networking on a global scale, the third-wave companies in university research parks are different animals altogether. They have a more open approach to research and a more interconnected view of the world. A conventional business park won't do the trick. Proximity to a big high-tech company — a software developer, for example — isn't so important, because the big companies are sending their operations overseas. Like so many other folks in America today, these smaller high-tech companies are looking for proximity to a research institution that isn't going anywhere — a university, a private research lab, a federal installation such as the Sandia National Laboratory in New Mexico. (Sandia has recently spawned its own science and technology center.)

These companies are not so concerned about security. They can't afford separate canteens and fitness centers — but they need their dry-cleaning done quickly and conveniently.

This sheds new light on the stale debate about whether the 21st-century economy needs urban or suburban spaces. For almost a decade now, we have seen a pitched battle between those who believe that our economic engines lie in the "nerdistans" of suburban office parks and those who believe it lies in the loft-and-latte environment of hip urban neighborhoods.

As the world transitions from Microsoft to Google, the urban approach has been winning. The latest hot campus setting in Silicon Valley is not in Mountain View or Palo Alto — it's downtown San Jose, where small companies can plug into a neighborhood that comes ready-made with lofts, hotels, fitness centers and coffee shops.

Now the university research parks are getting the same idea — proximity to urban and recreational amenities are more important than ever. The Sandia Science and Technology Park isn't in an urban location, but it is laced with great outdoor recreation trails.

As it turns out, research parks are not necessarily an either-or thing. They don't have to be either nerdistans or urban hip. At the University of Arizona, for example, Martinizing is only the beginning. The tilt-up business park world of the '80s is still there for those who want it — and many do. But the U of A is going to build the urban hip world right next door.

The lessons here are not just for university research parks. They have a bearing on every community and developer trying to catch the next wave. Focus on the research institution that can't move to India. Build all the urban and recreational amenities that you can around it- -or help the institution move to an urban location where that stuff already exists. Give traditional suburban business park buildings to those who want them. And don't forget about Martinizing.

2006

Making

The Once And Future Factory Town

It's not every day that your hometown can teach you a useful economic development lesson. But in a world of rapid economic change, where places as well as products are recycled, the town I grew up in tells a pretty good story. It's a story about the wrenching transition of a small manufacturing city into — well, into a small manufacturing city.

Located in upstate New York some 30 miles west of Syracuse, Auburn is, as it has been for decades, a town of about 35,000 people. Traditionally, Auburn was the county seat and the center of commercial life for the surrounding dairy-farming area. But economically and socially, it revolved around the numerous engine shops and the carpet, shoe and rope factories along the Owasco River, as well as the tight- knit ethnic enclaves — Italian, Ukrainian and Polish — that had grown up around the plants.

The industrial decline of towns such as this is an all-too-familiar chapter in American economic history. One by one, the factories folded, went south or moved to the Third World. In Auburn, as elsewhere, it was bad news for people of all backgrounds, not just factory workers. The trend-setting industrial research laboratory that my grandfather founded in 1929 vanished along with the factory it served. In recent years, the once-thriving downtown real estate market has been so weak that the city's most magnificent bank building changed hands for the price of a nice single-family house.

Yet today, a half-century after the industrial decline began, Auburn has stabilized, and a new industrial sector is emerging from the wreckage. Old factories have been retooled and rebuilt to meet current needs. The locomotive plant where my father worked during World War II has been partially rebuilt to house a subsidiary of Bombardier Inc., the parent company of Ski-Doo. A cluster of small fiber-optic companies is thriving with Silicon Valley-style synergy. Today, manufacturing still makes up 18 percent of the Auburn job market, and- -along with a 180-year-old state prison — still provides the city's economic foundation.

When you ask city officials why Auburn is surviving, they point first to labor productivity. The children of the factory workers, they say, still know how to work. True enough, but there is more to it than that. Economic developers in places such as Auburn have learned how to roll with the punches. For one thing, they have learned to "sell" Auburn not just to industrial companies but also to their own residents — the productive workers who might otherwise follow the factories south. The biennial "Made in Auburn" trade show is largely designed, says one economic development official, to generate phone calls to relatives: "Hey, Bobby, you know what you're making down there in Huntsville? Well, they're making it right here in Auburn, too!"

The days of humming along on the strength of a dozen permanent factories are, of course, long gone. Now, keeping the jobs in town requires an endless effort to keep dozens of balls in the air at the same time. Factories, companies and even industrial sectors will come and go, often in the space of a few years. But that doesn't mean the jobs have to vanish, too.

For example, Auburn has been home to an air-conditioner plant for decades. In the past 15 years, the plant has been sold by Singer to the Snyder interests in Texas, combined by Snyder with McQuay International of Minneapolis, sold to a Malaysian investment group, and renamed several times. But the operation is still in Auburn.

The city was able to help with a new plant by using state financial incentives, plus its own secret weapon: a prime parcel of municipally owned industrial park — land that the city had once slated for a landfill expansion. Today, the new 400,000-square-foot McQuay plant does more than $100 million a year in sales and employs about 700 workers. Recently, McQuay even transferred marketing and engineering jobs from Minneapolis to Auburn as part of a corporate decentralization.

Auburn is not out of the woods yet. The downtown retail area is still struggling. The older parts of town have deteriorated as the factory- gate neighborhoods have broken up and the population has sprawled out into the countryside. And the economic developers are never quite sure whether the plant manager — or even the plant — will still be there tomorrow. "Nowadays, the manager comes from Mississippi, he's here for two years, he lives in Syracuse, and he doesn't really get involved in the life of the community," says Cynthia Aikman, one of the city's planners.

But the difference between the Auburn of 1998 and the Auburn of 1948 is that everyone realizes the whole is bigger than the parts. No one factory can break Auburn by leaving, as local leaders were convinced it could a half-century ago. Auburn remains a going concern, thanks to the faith of its own workers, the ability to tread water in a fluid economic environment, and the essence of the place itself.

1998

Even In Decline, Always Count Your Assets

Lockport is an old canal town some 20 miles east of Niagara Falls. It's an historic city that's been the Niagara County seat since the Erie Canal was built. It boomed in the 19th century when industries powered up new factories by tapping the canal's waters.

Today, Lockport is home to a big plant owned by Michigan-based Delphi Corp., where 6,000 mostly unionized workers labor for a company that has been a big supplier to General Motors. Delphi is the biggest manufacturing employer in Niagara County and one of the biggest in New York State. Last October, however, the company filed for Chapter 11 bankruptcy protection. Since then, it has been engaged in an acrimonious battle with the United Auto Workers over dramatic wage and benefit reductions. That leaves Lockport sitting on edge and fearing the loss of thousands of jobs.

If all of this sounds so 20th century, it's also the kind of story that has served as a wake-up call for the struggling Western New York region — Buffalo, Niagara Falls and the outlying counties between Buffalo and Rochester. Still struggling to emerge from close to 40 years of stagnation, the Buffalo-Niagara Falls area is finally getting its act together with a regional economic strategy, courtesy of the Erie- Niagara Regional Partnership. There are some good ideas floating around — and also some good lessons on how a struggling region should approach the good ideas. As usual, it begins with the region's assets.

The most obvious and eternal asset is Niagara Falls — one of the most compelling place names in the world, right up there with Hollywood and Wall Street. This makes tourism an obvious play, but Western New Yorkers are still debating exactly how to take advantage of the tourism idea.

Next come new developments. In early December, the Seneca Indians broke ground on a new casino near downtown Buffalo, stimulating a debate about whether this would simply empty the pockets of residents in the region or serve as an economic engine. This could go either way — a casino and nothing else would simply empty pockets. But the Buffalo waterfront has a spectacular view of Lake Erie, so if the casino can be surrounded by other compelling attractions, it might serve, like Niagara Falls, as part of the foundation.

Then there are the biosciences. New York State, like so many other states, has decided to play hardball in the biosciences game and has made Western New York the focus, largely because of the "meds and eds" assets in Buffalo, such as Roswell Park, a cancer research center. But competition against richer regions, such as Arizona, California, Texas and Georgia, is ferocious; in December, a leading researcher — the State University of New York's single highest-paid employee — defected to Georgia Tech.

And finally, there's still manufacturing. Not the labor-intensive 20th-century manufacturing that made the region rich decades ago but advanced, technology-driven 21st-century manufacturing.

When you put these assets down on paper, they may not seem very impressive. Not everybody has Niagara Falls, but everybody has a tourism strategy. Not everybody has world-class biosciences research institutions, but everybody has a "meds and eds" strategy. Not everybody has Lockport, but everybody has an idea about how to make manufacturing work in the 21st century. Pile that on top of an aging and stagnating population in a region with a lot of out-migration, and it can be hard to see the competitive advantage.

But the key in Western New York — as everywhere else — is not just to identify your assets but also to act strategically to take advantage of them. Buffalo's not going to win the worldwide biosciences "arms race" outright — not with California throwing $3 billion at stem-cell research or Arizona spending hundreds of millions of dollars to create a biotech research base in downtown Phoenix.

What Western New York can do is figure out how to use and combine these assets in ways no one else can. Where else, for example, is there a strong biosciences research base — focused on drugs and treatments to help people stay healthier longer — located in a region with such a rapidly aging population that will need and want these new products? Where else can the biosciences be combined with sophisticated manufacturing capacity? And with cheap hydroelectric power from — you guessed it — Niagara Falls.

Economic development in the late 20th century was about identifying your assets. But in the early 21st century it will be about taking the next step: figuring out what you can do with those assets that no one else can do. Buffalo, Niagara Falls and Lockport may be accustomed to thinking that they can't compete in the worldwide race for prosperity, but Western New York may be the best laboratory in the country for the new rules of economic development.

2006

Even China's Losing Manufacturing Jobs

In the midst of the urban decay of the 1960s, Cleveland's planning director, Norman Krumholz, came up with a radical idea about the role urban planners should play in declining communities. Rather than trying to create more growth, planners should simply assume that their job was to manage decline. Cities would continue to empty out, and planners should help provide a soft landing for those left behind and for the communities where they lived, rather than maintaining the fiction that the fate of urban communities could be turned around completely.

The Krumholz approach came to mind recently because of the sobering statistics on worldwide manufacturing employment provided by William A. Ward, director of the Center for International Trade at Clemson University. Examining the trends in factory jobs across the globe, Ward concludes that American communities shouldn't focus on keeping as many manufacturing jobs as they can. Rather, cities and regions should be clear-eyed about which components of the manufacturing chain they should shed in order to stay competitive and which components they should try to retain. In other words, when it comes to manufacturing, America should learn how to manage decline.

Underlying Ward's conclusions is statistical information that turns our popular understanding of manufacturing trends on its head. We in

America usually assume that our industrial heritage is slipping away from us because other countries — principally China — are stealing our manufacturing jobs. But the reality is somewhat different: Everybody is losing manufacturing jobs, because of both productivity increases and global shifts in demand from goods to services.

Although worldwide data must be cobbled together, Ward's best guess is that a decade ago approximately 172 million manufacturing jobs existed worldwide. Almost 60 percent of them — 100 million factory jobs — were in China. Ten percent of them — 17.2 million — were in the United States. So in 1995, China had six manufacturing jobs for every one job in the United States.

By 2002, Ward concludes, the world had seen a startling change. Globally, manufacturing jobs had declined by 12 percent to about 150 million. China had actually experienced a bigger decline than the rest of the world, losing 15 million to 20 million jobs. The U.S. experienced a proportional decline, from 17 million to 15 million.

But Ward's analysis goes one step further. He conducts a "job-shift analysis" — a measure of how many jobs should have been lost through productivity gains and how many should have been added through expansion of the economy. The United States, he concludes, lost around 40 percent of its manufacturing jobs due to productivity increases and 60 percent to foreign competition. China, on the other hand, should have added 5 million jobs; instead it was a huge loser. "China lost as many manufacturing jobs in those years as the U.S. possessed," Ward wrote in one recent article.

So, the reality is far different from our perception. Half of our manufacturing jobs are being lost because our economy is not growing as fast as our productivity increases. China isn't trying to steal our jobs. Rather, it is engaged in an effort to keep the manufacturing base it already has — because, despite China's stupendous economic expansion (8 percent in recent years), this expansion is being outstripped by even more stupendous increases in productivity.

What this means, from our point of view, is that a decline in manufacturing employment is inevitable, at least in the short run. We will never be able to keep up with China — not because China's workers are so cheap but because China is engaged in a desperate effort to expand the economy faster than productivity increases.

We can and should hang on to a manufacturing base, but it has to be the right manufacturing base, one that creates high-value-added products that can support U.S. wages and also takes advantage of clusters of suppliers, markets, labor force and so forth. In other words, we must accept decline and manage it strategically.

To those of us who grew up in the factory towns of the Northeast, this is no surprise. We stopped squawking long ago about the loss of jobs to other parts of the United States. We knew those jobs would drift from the South to Latin America to Asia. But now, the rest of the country — including the once-booming manufacturing areas in the South and Southwest — has to face this same reality. In that sense, all of America has become one big Rust Belt. And we can't bring back the golden days of manufacturing, whether it's the '40s in Detroit, the '70s in South Carolina, or the '90s in Arizona. It's time to move on.

2006

The New Farmland

Apparently even the post-industrial economy needs industrial land.

For a generation, there's been a trend nationwide of recycling industrial land — and even old industrial buildings — for other land uses. This has been especially true on the coasts, where high urban land costs have made all real estate development, but especially housing, vastly expensive. Industrial land is a tempting alternative for real estate developers of all kinds because the land is usually much cheaper than land zoned for other uses. It's quickly becoming the urban farmland of the 21st century: a large stock of cheap land that can easily be converted to housing and other urban uses.

Now there's a reverse trend. Cities are fearful that they won't be able to retain the land they need for future industry, and — kind of like farmland — they are taking steps to preserve this land stock. Curiously enough, this activity is most intense on the West Coast, in cities such as San Jose, San Francisco, Seattle and Los Angeles, which have a reputation for being on the cutting edge of the post-industrial economy.

In California's Bay Area, the three biggest cities, San Francisco, Oakland and San Jose all have adopted policies to protect industrial land from further conversion to housing. In San Jose, the city has permitted the conversion of 120 acres per year in the past few years. In Oakland, the city has taken steps to protect industrial land in West Oakland, the very neighborhood that former Mayor Jerry Brown lives in.

Meanwhile, Seattle is considering an ordinance that would limit the size of office and retail uses in industrial zones. In Los Angeles, both the city and the county are doing studies to identify which land should be retained for industry and which land could be converted to housing or mixed use.

Why is this happening? Because, as it turns out, industry is still pretty important to the post-industrial economy.

San Jose is not only the center of the world's high-tech brainpower. It's still a pretty important manufacturing center for computers, chips and so forth. And all the other cities mentioned above — Seattle, San Francisco, Oakland and Los Angeles — are port cities. That means they are focal points for the import-export economy and centers of goods movement, warehousing and distribution.

Here in Southern California, where I live, there is still a strong manufacturing base. But there's also an enormous, fast-growing import industry that has a ripple effect through our entire regional economy and our regional demand for land. Trains and trucks flow out of the Ports of Los Angeles and Long Beach brimming with goods from Asia. These products are then offloaded, stored, transferred and otherwise handled in a vast number of warehouses and distribution centers all over the region. Since the goods-movement infrastructure is already in place, there's also a vast flow of goods the other way — out of small factories and workshops onto the trucks and back down to the port, to be shipped to other countries.

In an odd way, all this industrial activity is the result of the post-industrial society. Americans sit at their computers and click-click-click their way through the consumer economy. A lot of pundits think of this as an economy without factories or trucks, but the opposite is true. It's all about goods and trucks. What we're doing while clicking, of course, is buying goods. Those goods have to be made somewhere in the world and delivered to our houses in trucks.

All of which means we still need industrial land, even in the most post-industrial cities. So industrial land has become the new farmland — necessary for the economy, if not always economically viable on its own.

Like farmers, the business and industrial leaders in our large cities often are politically conservative and frequently advocate a "get government out of the way" approach to public policy. Yet if government gets out of the way and the market operates on its own, the very land that these industrial leaders need for their prosperity, will — just like farmland — probably vanish.

What's emerging in industrial land is an uncomfortable hybrid: a heavy set of regulations designed to protect an economic asset controlled by a pretty conservative group of business owners. But in a dense urban environment, this is the kind of regulation that's sometimes required for capitalism to thrive.

2007

Romancing The Smokestack

Not long ago, Area Development magazine, one of the leading site and facilities location publications in the country, released the results of its 22nd annual survey of corporate executives. The results: Cost, speed and labor force matter. Quality-of-life issues don't. Incentive packages are important but need to be tailored to the situation.

Surprising as these results may seem, they are an accurate reflection of the views of corporate executives — at least in the manufacturing sector. Almost 90 percent of the executives who responded to the survey run manufacturing companies. And that alone reveals an often-overlooked nuance about economic development these days: It's not just about the new, knowledge-based economy.

The old economy is still really important. And while technological breakthroughs and increasing skill levels are ever more important in manufacturing, some things don't change. The key criteria for manufacturers and other old-economy sectors are not taken from the pages of a Richard Florida book. The quality of the symphony and the quantity of the gay bars doesn't compute. The cost of labor, access to the rail and highway system, and the speed with which plants can get built matters a lot.

Which is why we sometimes get conflicting messages about what it takes to create economic development success these days.

Different things matter to different types of companies. And although the Richard Florida-style creative companies — the ones that come up with technological breakthroughs and set the table for economic progress — want quality of life in spades, it's still the old-economy companies that actually make what we use.

And they need different things than their creative counterparts. According to Area Development, the six things manufacturing executives want the most — and they want these considerably more than they want anything else — are:

- Highway accessibility
- Low labor cost
- Cheap and available energy
- Skilled labor
- Low construction costs
- Available land

All of these things, except possibly skilled labor, are becoming harder and harder to come by in the booming metropolitan areas in the United States. These are the regions typically viewed as the winners in the nation's competition for top-level jobs — the ones that are capturing the research institutions and growth companies. And that creates an opportunity for the rest of the country.

To a surprising degree — headlines to the contrary — we still make a lot of stuff here in the United States. According to the National Association of Manufacturers, manufacturing still accounts for almost 12 percent of the nation's gross domestic product. This is down significantly from the 1990s, but that's mostly because other parts of the economy are growing faster, not because manufacturing is declining in absolute terms. There are still more than 300,000 manufacturing companies in the United States and they employ more than 13 million people.

The future of American manufacturing will probably be a story of increased productivity, although it is not likely to be a tale of increased employment. In many ways, factories are the new farms. They require lots of capital and technology but not nearly as many people as they used to. And there will still be a considerable amount of churn — obsolete plants will continue to shut down or retool. But this means that there will be great opportunity to recruit and retain manufacturing companies. The Area Development survey found that 34 percent of manufacturing companies had expanded their operations in the past year, while 13 percent had contracted.

That's why it makes sense for cities and states to understand specifically where they should position themselves in the economic development marketplace. Sure, everybody wants to be "the next Silicon Valley," and once a decade or so somebody actually succeeds in this great quest. But not every place is a San Jose, San Diego, Austin or Research Triangle — places with great universities, a highly educated workforce, and a cachet that keeps the venture capital flowing. Cities are likely to succeed if they're realistic about what they've got, and if they can differentiate themselves in important ways from the increasingly expensive and congested places that get all the cool "new economy" stuff.

If what you've got is highway access and land — and this is increasingly what most struggling cities have lots of — then that's what you should sell. Because, as the Area Development survey suggests, there are more folks out there looking for what you've got than you might think.

2008

Selling

Will Retail Still Rule?

In the very first column I ever wrote in this space, I described the "mall wars" that had broken out between the California town I live in and the neighboring towns along the local freeway. My point was that in America — with our wonderfully decentralized governmental system — economic development is an "every jurisdiction for itself" proposition.

But there was another point hidden beneath the description of the endless legal and political skirmishes along the freeway, and it was this: Here in the West, where property taxes are frowned on and income taxes are merely tolerated, the sales tax has achieved an almost mythic status among government officials. It may be regressive and unfair, but it's painless. Taxpayers "pay at the pump" and forget about it; in many cases, local voters perceive it as a tax levied mostly on somebody else. Some cities rely on the sales tax for 70 percent or more of their local revenue. Whole states rely on the sales tax to operate.

And in an environment where job growth can sometimes be taken for granted, "economic development" really means enhancement of the sales- tax base. The local economic development director often functions as little more than the minister of retail sales, serving as the emissary to major chain retailers. These folks broker deals to bring the retailers to the nearest freeway interchange deals that sometimes require them to give away land and urban renewal money and provide necessary infrastructure services to large retail companies, all with an eye on a retail-oriented economic development strategy.

That's one of the reasons local governments are scared of the impact that Internet sales will have on their tax base. It's not just that they fear losing their revenue base because of online retailing. It's because many of them will have to rethink their entire economic development strategy and, perhaps, simply "write off" huge investments they have made based on the assumption that bricks-and-mortar retailing will continue to dominate the economy. And so how the Internet tax war plays out will have a major role in determining future economic development strategies — especially for local governments in the South and West, where sales taxes are critically important.

For now, the federal ban on Internet sales taxes remains in place. In the future, there appear to be two choices: Give the federal government control over collecting and distributing the tax revenue, or feed the byzantine system of state and local tax policies into a giant computer and let the software designers figure it out. Either way, state governments and local officials are likely to have less direct control over their own tax policies. In this way, the future is likely to look a lot like the recent history of California under Proposition 13, where the state determines how the property tax is distributed and local governments spend a lot of their time lobbying state officials to tweak the allocation formula to their advantage.

There may be a silver lining to this dark cloud, and it has to do, ironically, with the very placelessness of the Internet economy.

From the beginning of commerce, market towns have always been more prosperous than the hinterlands around them, simply because of the many spinoff effects of being the location where transactions occur. This has always bred smugness in market towns and hostility in the hinterlands — especially when the resulting tax revenue has worked to the advantage of the market town, which has more revenue to provide public services.

Retail-oriented economic development strategies are simply a modern version of this same rivalry. Ministers of retail sales don't care where the customers or the products come from. All they care about is creating the physical location where transactions take place, because that is the only financial incentive a sales-tax system gives to a government entity. The result, unfortunately, has often been an economic development strategy that focuses on retailing but cares little about jobs in core industries, housing for workers and the other necessary underlying components for retail commerce.

However, in the world of the Internet, the market town ceases to exist. Buyers and sellers don't require a physical location in order to engage in a transaction. And that fact alters the whole question of who should benefit from the tax revenue generated by retailing. Since no town serves as the host of the transaction, the resulting revenue will have to reward towns that host the buyers and sellers. We already see this in the Internet tax wars: States often can levy taxes on e- retailers whose headquarters are located inside their boundaries.

In other words, the Internet may mean that towns will be rewarded with sales-tax revenue for creating housing where buyers live and sites where companies are actually located, rather than subsidizing shopping centers. And that would likely lead to a much more balanced and constructive economic development strategy in sales-tax-oriented areas. The only losers would be the ministers of retail sales, who would become expendable. But maybe that's one job we can do without.

2000

Big-Box Blues

For the past several months, the biggest news here in Southern California has been the supermarket strike. Fearing an invasion by non-unionized Wal-Mart, the three biggest supermarket chains in the region threatened to reduce medical benefits for unionized grocery clerks, many of whom make $18 per hour or more. Drawing a line in the sand, the grocery clerks walked out, leading to a strike that lasted through Thanksgiving, New Year's — and beyond.

The Southern California supermarket strike touched off a vigorous debate in Los Angeles about the underpinnings of the economy — the "race to the bottom" that leads corporations to seek the lowest-cost workers worldwide; and the resulting downward pressure on prices that will make it difficult for supermarket employers such as Vons, Ralphs and Albertsons to support unionized workers with good benefits. It's hard to know what the long-term impact of the Wal-Mart grocery invasion and the grocery clerks' strike will be, although an erosion of the supermarket chains' market share seems almost inevitable.

And that raises an issue for local governments throughout the nation: The race to the bottom may affect not only grocery clerks but cities that count on the tax revenue from their own residents' everyday activities, such as grocery shopping.

Local governments have been engaged in cutthroat competition for a decade or more in hopes of attracting "big-box" retailers — the Wal-Marts, Costcos and Home Depots of the world that generate huge retail sales by drawing from a huge market area. There's generally room for only one Wal-Mart and Home Depot in every market area, but in most states all of the sales tax goes to the city or jurisdiction where the store is located. So cities that capture a Wal-Mart or a Home Depot are big tax winners, often at the expense of their neighbors, whose residents leave town to spend money as a result.

Up to now, virtually every city has been able to count on some sales- tax revenue because local residents tend to do their everyday shopping close to home. This is true for a wide variety of retail goods — dry cleaning, drug stores, and so forth — but the biggest cash cow is the supermarkets. In many states, grocery items are exempt from sales taxes because they are staples of life. Nonetheless, because they are full-service operations, chain supermarkets are big sales-tax generators.

Large supermarket chains drove most local grocers out of business decades ago. Even though they are centrally owned by large corporations, they have remained community-oriented institutions. Most grocery shoppers traditionally won't drive more than 2 or 3 miles to buy groceries, and the rule of thumb in the business is that you'll find one supermarket for every 10,000 or so houses.

The result is that the taxes generated by supermarket sales — next to the house and the car, the biggest portion of the household budget — have usually stayed in the same community as the residents themselves. But, as the Southern California supermarket strike has illustrated, even that might be changing.

The reason is simple: In its new 100,000-square-foot-plus "superstores," Wal-Mart sells groceries. So do Costco, Target and a wide range of big-box retailers whose core business traditionally has not been food. As these chains play out traditional expansion opportunities — new stores in new communities — they are looking at groceries as the next big growth opportunity. And they are betting that they can get shoppers to cross city lines and buy groceries in a big-box setting — especially if they are already traveling 5, 10 or 20 miles to buy other discount goods.

Local governments have started to deal with the political fallout from this phenomenon, as unions and other big-box opponents seek to use land-use regulations to try to keep Wal-Mart and other big-box grocers from entering certain marketplaces. And the big-boxes are not shy about fighting back. In the racially mixed Los Angeles suburb of Inglewood, Wal-Mart has sought to overcome local opposition to a superstore by placing on the local ballot an initiative to allow the store to locate there. The initiative also calls for streamlining the permit approval process. There's little question that such tactics will continue.

For many cities, the next step will be more disturbing: a battle over their own residents' grocery money. They will have to compete with each other for grocery-enhanced big-box retailers that will attract grocery shoppers from all over a wide area. In other words, the age of the local supermarket might be ending and competition for the regional supermarket just beginning.

Over the past century, generation after generation of Main Street stores has been driven out of business by ever-larger and more efficient corporate retailers. In pursuing their own economic development goals, local governments have at least been able to hang on to the tax revenue generated by basic day-to-day activities. But now, cities can no longer take even the milk money for granted.

2004

The Dying Auto Mall

Over the past two decades, the funding of local government has become increasingly intertwined with the sale of cars. Governments live off of sales taxes more than ever before, and — except for the occasional RV or boat — no single consumer product generates more sales tax revenue than a car. That's why car dealers and local governments have increasingly gone into business together to create auto malls.

But the auto mall may now be a dinosaur. The car business is temporarily in the tank, of course. But the current depression in auto sales is likely to create a more permanent contraction in the number of franchise auto dealerships in the United States — and browsing for cars has shifted dramatically to the Internet.

So local governments that have laid a big bet on auto malls in the past few years have a choice. They can either play defense, in the hope that by helping, protecting or even subsidizing their auto retailers, they can retain a larger share of a diminishing market. Or they can play offense and try to figure out what comes next — both in auto retailing and in the reuse of the land that the auto malls currently take up.

This restructuring is pretty similar to the reshuffling we saw a few years ago in regional malls that sell general merchandise. Well into the 1990s, regional malls were viewed as unassailable retail fortresses.

Localities that had them were sitting pretty; those that didn't have them wanted them.

Then consumer tastes changed, and, in particular, the market bifurcated. People generally wanted either an upscale retail "experience," or they wanted discount goods. Those who opted for the "experience" went to boutique shops on a trendy downtown street or to an upscale open-air lifestyle center similar to a downtown. Those who wanted cheap goods went to a big-box "power center." This left most regional malls — ill-equipped to serve either preference — out in the cold. Many closed or contracted or morphed into some other function: They began hosting city halls, libraries, even megachurches.

The California beach town where I live played defense in the mall wars, subsidizing a consolidation of department stores into one big mall. We "defeated" our neighboring city, which lost its mall. But that failed enterprise was soon replaced with a very strong power center containing everything from Home Depot to Borders. In retrospect, I'm not sure winning the mall war really was a victory, after all.

Now we see a similar transition in the auto industry. Car dealerships, like department stores, are closing. More and more, people are scouring the Internet for cars and finding alternatives — used car dealers, fleet sales, and wholesalers willing to reach out to the general public. Among auto malls, there will be "winners" and "losers." But, as with regional shopping centers, it's not entirely clear whether the winners will be those who protect their auto malls, or those who lose them.

In the short term, the cities that succeed in keeping their auto malls will retain much of their sales tax base. But their success is likely to come at a higher cost than in the past, because competition among cities for dealers is going to increase. The dealers who are still in business will hold out for bigger subsidies, and communities will likely provide them.

The places that lose their auto malls altogether will take a short-term revenue hit, but they may be presented with a long-term opportunity: redevelopment of high-profile retail land along the freeway.

Perhaps the best option for many local governments is to go after something innovative. The whole idea of the auto mall is that it is a destination people are willing to travel a long distance to visit, because they can browse so many dealerships at once. But if people can browse on the Internet, the destination value of auto malls vanishes. So cities might be well advised to figure out how to pair the remaining auto dealerships with other possible "destination" activities, so that instead of being stand-alone destinations, auto malls are one component of a multi-faceted strategy.

This could mean pairing auto dealerships with entertainment or recreational venues, which also benefit from freeway locations. Or it could mean creating whole new packages, such as adding the hybrid-only used car dealership or a "theme" retailer. The bottom line is that, with cars, as with so many other products, simply offering them for sale no longer will be enough to get customers in the door.

2009

Moving

More Airports Than We Need

All around the country, a new airport craze is in full swing. Denver International is finally running smoothly — the first major airport built since Richard M. Nixon was president. Big airports coast-to- coast are expanding rapidly. New ones are being constructed, including speculative gambles such as MidAmerica Airport in St. Clair County, Illinois — 25 miles from St. Louis — and Northwest Arkansas Regional Airport, near Fayetteville. And so many military bases are closing that airfield dreams are popping up everywhere. In Southern California, which already has four major airports, plans are being made to create at least four more out of closed bases.

Could we be overdoing it? Maybe. A few years ago, the conventional wisdom was that the demand for airport space would not be satisfied in the foreseeable future. Airline patronage was growing fast, while local opposition was making it almost impossible to build new airports or expand existing ones.

Now, it seems, we may be on the verge of a glut. The massive Denver airport has only one hub airline so far — United — whereas the city's old Stapleton Field had three. MidAmerica in Illinois is fully operational, but no commercial airlines use it, and it has no scheduled flights. Northwest Arkansas may be in the same situation when it opens. If you build it, is it possible that they won't come?

Well, yes. The whole role of airports in economic development appears to be more complicated and harder to nail down than anyone thought. On the one hand, communities want to invest in airports in order to stimulate economic activity. On the other hand, merely having an airport may not be enough. "In a deregulated airline industry," says Roger Cohen, a spokesman for the Air Transport Association, "airlines fly to markets, not airports."

So, far from being a "field of dreams" issue, airport construction may well be a chicken-and-egg question involving the airport and the surrounding market. If you want to promote growth, which do you subsidize: the chicken or the egg?

Much of the airport jostling these days derives from typical American decentralization. Commercial air travel is required to operate as a seamless system under the guidance of the Federal Aviation Administration, but when and where to schedule the flights is up to the airlines. And where the airports are is up to the local communities — at least partly. Right now, cities, metropolitan areas and states all over the country have decided it is in their interest to subsidize airport construction and expansion.

In some cases — as with the pending expansion of Los Angeles International Airport — the market for air travel is so extensive that there probably will never be too much capacity. But in other cases, as with MidAmerica, airports turn out to be little more than another way for communities to fight it out.

Lambert St. Louis International Airport, for example, is small and outdated, but it's a well-established destination for Southwest, Delta, United, American and its flagship airline, TWA. Lambert is undergoing a $2.6 million expansion that is scheduled for completion in seven years.

Meanwhile, just across the state line, St. Clair County in Illinois has constructed MidAmerica at a cost of $300 million. County officials say they aren't worried about the lack of commercial business right now, because they've budgeted for a five-year ramp-up period. But there's little question that the Lambert-MidAmerica battle is a less- than-ideal (if typical) solution to a regional problem. After fighting for decades over which state would get the new St. Louis airport, Missouri and Illinois decided they would each build one — even though there was little evidence of sufficient demand to support two.

Local leaders often say that building airports is a local decision and so there's nothing wrong with communities wasting their own money if they feel like it. But many airports are constructed with substantial amounts of federal money, and one could argue that federal priorities should prevail.

In the case of MidAmerica, some $150 million, or fully half the construction budget, came from the FAA as a result of the fact that Illinois won the lobbying battle in Washington. Because MidAmerica is a "joint use" operation with Scott Air Force Base, the Pentagon chipped in another $60 million. But this did not stop Missouri from using Lambert's established position to raise revenue from passengers and from Missouri taxpayers to expand Lambert — thus going into competition with the federal government's own decision to funnel money to Illinois rather than Missouri.

Maybe the lesson in all this isn't that if you build something, people will come, or even that you need to decide between the chicken and the egg. Maybe it's just that in a decentralized system such as the one we have in the United States, you can't stop communities from taking big gambles even if they're destined to lose. It's not likely that both Lambert and MidAmerica will come out winners in the end — but it would have been impossible to talk either side out of taking the gamble in the first place.

1998

Angel At The Airport

For somebody who travels a lot, I live a long way from any airport. From my house, it's 45 miles to Santa Barbara, where regional jets can whisk me quickly (though expensively) to places like Salt Lake City and Denver. It's 60 miles to Burbank, where Southwest Airlines takes me up and down California on a regular basis. And it's 70 miles — and a lot of hassle — to flights out of Los Angeles, which can take me anywhere in the world.

I live in an affluent county of 800,000 people, so you'd think I would have a better alternative closer to home. But somehow it doesn't work out that way. There's no jet service anywhere in my county. Although it's only a 10-minute drive to Oxnard Airport, once I'm at that tiny facility all I can do is fly on United to LAX. The runway at Oxnard is littered with the carcasses of small regional airlines that have failed in their attempts to lasso us locals and take us to regional hubs such as San Francisco, Las Vegas and Phoenix.

So as a traveler I felt a little envious recently when I read about Wichita's "Fair Fare$" effort, designed to bring low-cost airlines into Wichita's relatively small market. Wichita's problem was not a lack of air service but a lack of cheap air service. Major air carriers serve Wichita, but fares are so high that Wichitans regularly drive three or four hours to Kansas City and other major air markets to save money.

In response, Wichita did something no city had ever done before: It provided AirTran, a discount air carrier, with a subsidy of $5 million. The city agreed to subsidize AirTran up to $3 million the first year and $1.5 million the second year; to hold AirTran harmless for the fuel cost increases; and to pay for AirTran's advertising campaign.

The result is a mixed bag so far. Wichita has cheaper air service now. Other discount airlines have entered the market, and prices have gone down a lot. But at the same time, AirTran is chewing through the public subsidy faster than anyone expected, and there has been considerable public controversy about the tactic.

The basic question in the Wichita air service situation is the same one that underlies so many economic development decisions: Which pieces of economic infrastructure are so essential to a city or a region that they must be maintained — even at public expense — if the market does not provide them? You can ask this same question not only about air service (or cheap air service) but also about convention centers, sports teams, airports, rail service, job skills and so on.

This has become a more difficult question in recent years because the federal government has largely withdrawn from the debate (even though it still provides much of the money). Going back almost 200 years — to the transcontinental railroad and before — the federal government has usually proven willing to pay, cajole, influence and sometimes even force private businesses to create and maintain this infrastructure. But in the past 20 years or so, things have changed.

One of my most vivid memories as a young reporter was attending a meeting of the Civil Aeronautics Board in Washington, D.C., back in 1979. As I watched the board's chairman, Alfred Kahn, implement his vision of economic deregulation of airlines, I didn't realize the magnitude of what he was up to. By eliminating the regulatory requirements that airlines serve certain markets at certain prices, he was laying the foundation for efforts such as Wichita's today. If we do not have a national policy that forces internal subsidies within industries such as airlines, then cities and regions will use anything they can dream up to get what they think they need — or they will risk falling behind in the ruthless economic game that we play in the United States.

Since state and local governments can't effectively regulate national industries, it's no surprise that they will use subsidies in all kinds of creative ways, including giving direct payments to individual companies they want. Over the years, I've generally argued that it's a bad idea to lay all your chips on an individual business, and that cities and states are better off investing in the assets required for any business to succeed — the transportation system, the labor force. After all, you can't guarantee how the market will respond to any individual business' products.

But are some industries so vital and so concentrated that they're different? Is there no other way to get good air service at a good price than to simply subsidize the airlines directly? Maybe, thanks to Alfred Kahn, it's the only way to get the job done. Or maybe the Wichita gambit can best be viewed as a way to prime the pump: Stimulate latent air travel demand in Wichita with lower prices. After all, Southwest and other discount airlines have done this all over the nation in larger markets. Maybe Wichita can do the same, and then remove the subsidy when the market is booming.

2002

The New Urbanist Airport

The successful airports of the 20th century were serious economic engines of the first order. Starting life as airstrips in the 1920s, they eventually became major travel hubs, typically surrounded by industrial buildings, convention hotels and even office complexes. Unlike the cities they serviced, however, they were distinctively suburban in nature: auto-oriented land hogs, built on the assumption that land was abundant and cheap.

The successful airports of the 21st century will be different. For one thing, they will have to operate within a crowded and increasingly urban fabric. It's unlikely that any brand-new airports will be built. Only two have been constructed in the past 40 years — in Dallas-Fort Worth and Denver. The future is likely to focus on incremental expansion — cramming more things in and around airport properties and working more closely with surrounding communities and jurisdictions to make airports compatible.

Which raises an interesting question: Why are airports so auto-oriented? After all, it's one of the few situations in American society where absolutely everybody leaves their car behind. All airline passengers spend a great deal of time as pedestrians. At an increasing number of airports, they become rail passengers, too, just to get from their gate to the terminal.

So, tens of thousands of people are traveling around and to airports without their cars every day. This ought to be a New Urbanist dream. And, according to airport experts, this is probably how airports will evolve in the decades ahead.

John Kasarda, the University of North Carolina business professor who coined the term "aerotropolis," says that in order to be economically successful in the future, airports cannot afford to follow the "spontaneous, haphazard" development pattern of the past few decades. Because airports are congested and running out of land — and because more and more of their patrons will be arriving without cars — these new, high-end business centers will have to be nodal and mixed-use. They may lack housing because of noise considerations, but they are going to have to provide air travelers with many business services in a compact setting — and these services will have to be easily accessible without a car. In other words, the successful 21st-century airport will be a New Urbanist economic engine.

As airports expand in crowded conditions, they are going to have to work more closely with their neighbors. The key will be doing more comprehensive land use planning that involves areas within the airport's boundaries, as well as on property known in the airport business as "outside the fence."

Most airports are focused on "doing a plan that meets FAA regulations inside the fence," says consultant Mark Bowers, who has been working on a commercial development plan for Dallas-Forth Worth International Airport. DFW's plan was done in collaboration with four surrounding cities and is increasingly focused on the smart-growth approaches planners love. The DART Orange Line light rail to DFW is scheduled to open in 2013, and contains an important stop — Belt Line Road — just outside the fence. Bowers says that DART was originally imagining Belt Line as primarily a park-and-ride location, but now is reconsidering the possibility of a mixed-use center, one that would be easily accessible from the airport terminals, as well as from other nearby business centers such as Las Colinas, which also will be on the Orange Line.

DFW itself will focus on centralized business centers that provide "valet services," such as auto repair and dry cleaning. That way, travelers can drop their car and use their legs and various rail-transit lines to run their errands and get to the terminal.

The "aerotropolis" notion is partly dependent on the assumption that demand for air travel will continue to increase and there will be an ongoing need to expand airports in the future. Not everybody believes that this pressure will materialize. The recent climb in fuel prices has clearly dampened travel demand and put many airlines in a tough spot.

Either they can increase prices significantly, thus cutting ridership, or they can eat the fuel cost, thus eliminating profitability.

It may well be that air-travel demand will level off as fuel prices continue to rise. But even if it flattens, airports will continue to serve as critical business hubs for the nation's economy. And that means the New Urbanist airport is likely to emerge.

2008

The Fedex Story

Deep inside a huge warehouse-like building on the grounds of Memphis International Airport lies the Federal Express Corp.'s "primary matrix." It is a spider web of 80 conveyor belts that churn at different levels, perpendicular to one another.

Every weekday night, a million packages arrive in Memphis on more than 150 FedEx cargo flights. They are loaded, by hand, onto the top rack of belts. Then they are nudged, prodded and dropped by computerized robot arms onto the lower rack of belts, where they move in groups toward the proper outbound plane.

The packages start arriving at 10 p.m. By 6 a.m., they're all gone.

FedEx has other sorting hubs around the country, but Memphis remains the largest. As company officials like to say, Memphis is the location of last resort for any package that missed the cutoff times for flights into other airports.

On the ground, the process of sorting these packages and moving them out is accomplished by an army of workers and such a vast fleet of vehicles that you would think only Dwight Eisenhower could have dreamed it up. In fact, of course, this enormous sorting and shipping operation was dreamed up by a man named Fred Smith, who wrote the idea up for a business-school term paper and — undeterred by a low grade— proceeded to make it a success in the real world.

The FedEx story has been told over and over again in business schools and management seminars around the world. Less often discussed, however, is the business location decision that helped to make it happen.

In 1973, Smith agreed to relocate the then-fledging Federal Express company from Little Rock to Memphis International Airport. It is arguable that this was the single most important economic development decision made in any major U.S. city in the past 30 years. Today, Memphis International Airport, which serves the 42nd-largest metropolitan area in the United States, is the busiest cargo airport in the world. The freight volume in Memphis is 30 percent higher than in Los Angeles and Miami, 50 percent higher than at Kennedy Airport in New York and double that of London Heathrow. Almost 10,000 people in the Memphis area work for Federal Express, and it's estimated that one in five workers in Memphis works in air-related operations. Federal Express is the lifeblood of Memphis.

So it's worth pondering just exactly why Federal Express is located in Memphis — and what it takes to keep it there.

Smith liked Memphis for a bunch of reasons. First, and maybe most important, it was his hometown. Second, the airport had good weather. And third, it was in the Central Time Zone — meaning that without relocating to the East Coast, FedEx could buy an extra hour and still be close to most of the nation's major markets.

But over time, the way Memphis approached its airport — and its relationship to FedEx — turned out to be just as important. In the 1960s, you couldn't even land jets in Memphis. According to one airport authority old-timer, FedEx was lured in part by a $6 million loan from the airport, which was looking for a cargo anchor at an airfield that served only 30 planes a day at the time. It was part of an overall expansion plan, which also included the opening of a 9,300- foot runway in 1972.

It was a risky move. After all, who could have predicted that overnight delivery would turn into such a big business? But today Memphis is still investing in FedEx. The airport is in the process of completing an 11,000-foot runway at a cost of $100 million, and the principal beneficiary will once again be FedEx, which will be able to fly cargo planes nonstop to other continents.

The main lesson of the Memphis experience, of course, is that size — metropolitan size, that is — doesn't matter. In fact, in many ways, large size would have been a hindrance to Federal Express. The company needed the runways to be clear all night long, and that wouldn't have happened in Los Angeles or New York.

There is also the issue of lighter traffic in a smaller metropolitan area. FedEx trucks from throughout the Mid-South bring packages to the Memphis airport, so that Memphis' relatively minor traffic problems are a plus for the company. That wouldn't be the case in a Los Angeles or New York.

The main drawback for Memphis — a theoretical one, at this point — is that the city has laid too many chips on one company. Who knows whether FedEx will survive in 30 years?

But in the long run, that may not matter. The original loan notwithstanding, Memphis has put most of its money over the years into the airport, not into the company. Today, Memphis has the facilities, the labor pool and the reputation. And last year, when UPS decided to open its first combined air-ground sorting facility, it chose Memphis as the location. So even if FedEx goes out of business someday, Memphis' FedEx gamble will have paid off anyway.

2000

Winners And Losers Along The Alameda Corridor

It may be hard to believe that Los Angeles has a Rust Belt, but it's not hard to find. All you have to do is head down Alameda Street out of downtown L.A. For most of its 30 miles, Alameda is the classic industrial street — bisected by rail lines, lined with scrap-metal businesses and filled with so much truck traffic that the asphalt is eternally chewed to pieces.

For 70 years, the area around this corridor has more resembled Detroit or Akron than Beverly Hills. In its heyday, life in southeast L.A. County revolved around Firestone and General Motors and Uniroyal and the union halls that surrounded them. As the social critic Mike Davis once wrote, the southeast area represented "a happy ending to `The Grapes of Wrath'" for the Dust Bowl immigrants who populated the area.

Today, all these plants are gone, and the aircraft and missile plants are barely hanging on. And that's why southeast L.A. County is becoming a laboratory for two competing economic development philosophies — what Edward Blakely, dean of the School of Urban and Regional Planning at the University of Southern California, has called the "corporatist" and "community" approaches.

Corporatists look at the region as a whole, and simply try to make the pie bigger without worrying about distribution. Community advocates worry about equity and try to slice the pie a different way, sometimes without concern for whether it's getting bigger. There's a case for each in southeast L.A. County.

The burden of the area's problems has fallen disproportionately on minority groups. The area has many historically black neighborhoods, and there's also a burgeoning Latino population. Today the area, which has about 1.7 million people, has the lowest incomes, educational levels and homeownership rates of any area in the West.

Now, however, the Los Angeles area sees Alameda as the lifeline to economic recovery. Alameda Street is the biggest bottleneck in an otherwise fast-moving transportation system that ships goods from the booming ports of Los Angeles and Long Beach to distribution points throughout the country. Under a plan promoted by the region's economic development leaders, a depressed "freeway" carrying rail and truck traffic would be built at a cost of $1.8 billion along the Alameda Corridor for some 20 miles between the ports and the major rail yards near downtown L.A.

But the political landscape of southeast L.A. County is cut in a different pattern than the economic landscape, and that is where this tale of economic development becomes complicated. The cities of Los Angeles and Long Beach are not the only players in this drama. In typical suburban fashion, southeast L.A. County is cut up into 27 different cities. Some are industrial cities, such as Vernon, that have many businesses and almost no residents. Some are historically black suburbs, such as Compton. Some are small residential cities, such as Huntington Park, that are now mostly Latino. And some, such as Downey, are traditional suburbs reeling from the aerospace cutbacks.

To try to bring the area back, the southeast L.A. County cities have banded together to pursue a common economic development agenda. But it is not easy. The Alameda Corridor has raised the classic economic development question of who will truly benefit from this public investment. "What everybody's afraid of," says Gill Hicks, director of the Alameda Corridor Transportation Authority, "is that we're going to spend $1 billion and all the jobs are going to go to Texas."

Where you stand on this issue depends more on your view of the world than on the situation of your city. For example, Huntington Park City Councilman Raul Perez, a Mexican immigrant who represents one of the poorest cities in the area, is strongly behind the corridor, saying it will revive the entire area. That's the classic corporatist view. Paul Richards, the African-American mayor of the equally depressed adjacent city of Lynwood, is more skeptical. "We have to ask the question of who wins and who loses," he insists. The Corridor advocates, says this classic promoter of the community view, fail to ask the question of whether the rising tide will, indeed, lift all boats.

Most regional economic development efforts like the Alameda Corridor get caught in the vise of this debate sooner or later. It can be a destructive debate. But it's also necessary. The fault line between rich and poor is growing — and in America's metropolitan areas, this division is being played out geographically as areas like southeast L.A. County get left behind. No longer can economic leaders simply assume that economic growth will create a middle-class paradise. Along Alameda Street, as in other American cities, it will take a lot of work to make sure that "El Norte" has as happy an ending as "The Grapes of Wrath."

1996

The 21St Century Ltd.

Earlier this spring, the first freight train emerged from an underground trench a few miles south of downtown Los Angeles and headed along a separate right of way toward the enormous rail yards east of the city's business areas.

This is the kind of event that would seem to be a major breakthrough of the 19th century, not the 21st. Nonetheless, the switch giving the freight train the green light was pulled by here-and-now political leaders — U.S. Transportation Secretary Norm Mineta, California Governor Gray Davis and Los Angeles Mayor James Hahn, among others — and it was done in front of a crowd of more than 1,000 people.

In general, the politicians heralded the opening of the Alameda Corridor with the kind of rhetoric ordinarily reserved for space launchings and freeway openings. Davis compared the debut of the freight corridor to the opening of the transcontinental railroad. U.S. Representative David Dreier called it "the silk road of the 21st century."

This rhetoric might be a bit extreme. But like so many other projects around the country right now, the Alameda Corridor is a prime example of the most important kind of economic development projects our metropolitan areas will see in the 21st century: filling in the missing piece. That is, streamlining an existing system rather than creating a new one.

The deal to put the corridor together was complicated and expensive. It's a $2.2 billion project that required the combined efforts of dozens of federal, state and local agencies, as well as two major railroads, Burlington Northern Santa Fe and Union Pacific. Given the range of players involved, it's not surprising that it took more than 20 years to bring the project to fruition, with five years for construction alone.

Underneath all the complexity, however, the Alameda Corridor is a very simple idea. It is an enormous trench — 50 feet wide, 33 feet deep and 10 miles long — combined with a series of bridges, overpasses and underpasses at either end to create a separate, 20-mile-long right of way for freight

Its purpose is also simple. The corridor is designed to slice through one of the most crowded and congested parts of Los Angeles and remove one of the biggest roadblocks to the efficient movement of goods in the United States: the gap between the containerized ports in the Long Beach area and the transcontinental railroad system that begins in downtown Los Angeles.

There has been a lot of debate over the years about whether the poor, mostly Latino communities along the corridor would share in its economic benefits. The presence of the rail lines helped to create southern Los Angeles County as an industrial powerhouse, but it also has put these communities in the path of pollution, noise and danger. Throughout the corridor's planning, these communities feared that they would bear the brunt of more train traffic and yet miss out on the resulting jobs — an on-going concern that has been a matter of debate for more than six years.

Today, there are still outposts of community opposition to the corridor, but they are rare. In the end, most elected officials along the corridor bought into the project — partly because construction included local hiring and apprenticeship programs, but mostly because of the trench.

When the corridor opened in April, elected officials repeatedly crowed about the local hiring — even though, given the fact that the project cost more than $2 billion, the numbers were rather small. Overall, 1,200 local residents were hired to construct the corridor, and 600 entered union apprenticeship programs.

The physical impact on the communities is more profound. By boxing the trains in and pushing them below street level, the trench transformed the corridor into the railroad equivalent of a flood- control project — a project that protects communities from the adverse effects of a corridor rolling through their neighborhoods. For most of its length, the trench isn't pretty. It's a large, depressed box of concrete along Alameda Street, fenced off so no one can enter it. In keeping with the flood-control theme, it looks a lot like the channelized Los Angeles River.

The unattractiveness of the project doesn't seem to bother local politicians. For them, the trench is far preferable to an endless series of freight trains snaking along the edge of their town.

Like most American cities today, Los Angeles is no longer a free-wheeling place with plenty of room to grow. Like the trains along the Alameda Corridor, it is boxed in. In Los Angeles — as in Boston, New York, Chicago and elsewhere — the future of economic development lies not in building brand-new things. Rather, it lies in filling in the gaps and making existing systems more efficient by providing the missing pieces. As the Alameda Corridor proves, the missing piece doesn't have to be grandiose or beautiful to do the job. It just has to work.

2002

Partnering

The Rural Metropolis

Not long ago, I sat down to lunch with all of the planning directors and economic development specialists in Redding, California, an important town at the northern end of California's Sacramento Valley, not far from the Oregon border. The Redding area has suffered from sluggish economic growth in recent years, and for close to two hours these local officials took turns telling me about the troubles their community faced and the "assets" they had to work with in confronting them.

The list of these "assets" contained no great surprises — at least not at first. There was beautiful countryside, cheap housing (compared with the rest of California, at any rate), recreational opportunities at nearby Lake Shasta and a stable work force. "And, of course, we have a state university with a good reputation," one of the planning directors said. "That's a great help." All the others nodded in agreement.

I looked up from my pasta, perplexed. I had spent the better part of two days touring Redding, and I had seen no educational institution more substantial than a community college. "Where?" I asked. "What university?" And then they explained. The school they were referring to was the California State University campus in Chico — set against the western foothills of the Sierra Nevada, 75 miles away.

It had never occurred to me before that a college in one city might be part of the economic foundation of another city. But in fact, it makes perfect sense. As a smaller town located in a rural area, Redding will probably never have all the big-ticket items a city needs if it is going to compete effectively in the modern economy. But it's not really Redding that's competing. It's the whole northern part of the Sacramento Valley: Redding, Chico and a whole string of other towns that are interrelated economically. We live in the age of the region, not the age of the city.

Urban policy wonks have been telling us this for a while now. Bill Barnes and Larry Ledebur of the National League of Cities say that the whole idea of a "national" economy has become outmoded, and we need to focus instead of the idea of a "common market" among regional economies, throughout the nation and the world. Other experts have focused on industry "clusters" — emphasizing the point that in a fast- moving, rapidly changing global economy, companies can't be isolated in "company towns" the way they once were. They must be located in close geographical proximity to each other, so they can work together to keep themselves competitive on a global basis.

The lesson in all this for students of economic development ought to be obvious. If regions are the new building blocks of the world economy — if it is the region that matters, not the nation or the city or the state — then it is the region that should also be the locus of economic development policy.

The problem, of course, is that the economic power and political power don't always reside at the same address. As the economic notion of "global regionalism" suggests, the geography required for vibrant economic combinations to succeed is always changing. Yet the boundaries of political jurisdictions are, by and large, staying the same. We aren't in the business of creating new states, cities or counties, or redrawing the lines to reflect demographic change. So New York fights with New Jersey over one set of table scraps from the regional economy, and Philadelphia battles with its suburbs over a different set of scraps.

It doesn't have to be that way. If our country functions as an economic "common market" among interlocking regions, as Barnes and Lebedur suggest, then different cities — and even different states — would do well to pursue strong multilateral diplomacy, just as countries do.

Charles Royer, who served two terms as mayor of Seattle, tells a story about the annual leadership conference he used to organize for an elite group of business and political leaders in his community. Every year, as they came to deal with larger and larger economic issues, they widened their net to include officials from a broader area — Tacoma, Olympia, even the city of Vancouver, across the border in British Columbia. "We knew we had really gotten it right," he recalls, "when we decided we should hold our annual Leadership Conference not in Seattle, but in Boise, Idaho. Because when we talk about economic development in Seattle — well, Boise is a big reason why we have a port."

You have to swallow a lot of pride in order to think this way and understand what role your community might really play in creating a strong regional economy. After all, this nation is filled with Chicos that don't want to associate with Redding, and Seattles that want nothing to do with Boise. And going against that territorial instinct can sound like political suicide to a lot of local officials. But any successful business owner will tell you that if you want to get rich, you can't be too haughty about what your product is or the customers you sell it to. The future belongs to the politicians who understand that Chico is a part of Redding and Seattle is a part of Boise — and all these combinations are part of regional economies that will be rich at home only to the extent that they can sell successfully to the rest of the world.

1999

Leveraging Rural Resources

Margaretville, New York, is the kind of place where different worlds meet. Located in rural Delaware County, 140 miles northwest of Manhattan, it's a small town where you'll hear both upstate and downstate accents, where you'll see a pickup truck arriving from the country and find a menorah in an antique-store window.

It turns out that Margaretville is also the kind of place where the economy and the environment meet. It's now the headquarters of the Catskill Watershed Corp., one of the largest new economic development organizations anywhere in the country, staked with $60 million from the New York City Department of Environmental Conservation. With this stake, Margaretville and the Catskills are going to try to take their status as a resource colony of a large metropolis — a status all too common in rural America — and transform it into economic success.

The $60 million came because New York City is connected to the Catskills by water — specifically, by a series of reservoirs and aqueducts all over the Catskills that collect and deliver water to millions of people downstate. Over the decades, upstate-downstate relations have been rocky, to say the least. But the two sides recently reached an historic accord when the U.S. Environmental Protection Agency accepted New York's proposal to maintain water quality with $1 billion worth of clean-water improvements in the Catskills, rather than spending $6 billion for a water filtration plant.

The rural Catskill towns went along with the deal, which includes construction of septic systems and wastewater plants, along with a retrofit of the stormwater system. But part of the price was for the city to finance the Catskill Fund for the Future, a $60 million regional economic development program. "We were just looking for economic justice in the watershed," says Tony Bucca, town supervisor in Hunter, New York, and a ringleader among the Catskill local officials who negotiated the deal, "so we became legal terrorists in a way. We let it be known to the New York City Department of Environmental Protection that without a substantial economic development package, there'd be no settlement."

As a result, the Catskill Watershed Corp., a regional organization that administers the Catskill end of the watershed agreement, is now sitting on one of the biggest economic development piles in the country. All the money resides in Margaretville under the control of the CWC.

Two years ago, when the CWC was first set up, Tony Bucca predicted that the organization would be besieged by groups arguing that a whole variety of social and cultural activities should be considered economic development. Instead, the corporation commissioned a team of economic consultants to create a "blueprint" for economic development. The blueprint, approved by the CWC in June, suggested focusing on four areas: revitalization of the region's villages; tourism and the arts; agriculture, forestry and mining; and manufacturing.

None of these four categories are unusual in and of themselves. But all have been given a rural Catskill slant. Rather than gunning for big business, the Catskills will go after small niches in all these areas. The Main Street revitalization, for example, is considered necessary to draw entrepreneurs who want a livable small-town lifestyle. Manufacturing efforts are likely to focus on specialty manufacturing that spins off the region's artisans. And agriculture and mining activities will target such niche items as organic farming, for which the market in New York is growing, and bluestone quarries, which do not harm water quality as much as heavy mining normally does.

But even as the CWC seeks to focus on "hard" economic development issues, "soft" problems are also arising. For example, says Alan Rosa, the CWC's executive director, niche entrepreneurs looking for quaint small towns need good employees. Currently, he adds, "we don't have the laborers to support a lot of these businesses. A lot of the people here do not have the best work ethic in the world. That's what happens when you depend a lot on tourism and low-paying jobs." So the fund for the Catskills may wind up dealing with social issues simply as a means of achieving economic ends.

It's hard to say whether Alan Rosa and his $60 million fund will succeed in nurturing economic success in the Catskills. But it's already paid off in terms of regional cooperation. It has helped to heal the severe split in the region between the rural, upstate- oriented north and southern areas closer to New York City. In a way, the Catskill Watershed Corp. is a regional equivalent of an inner-city community development corporation — created by local protesters who eventually realized that they had to cross the line from protest to active entrepreneurship to get things done. "If you operate at a regional level," Rosa says, "the results will be much greater."

1999

Local Hero V. Regional Champ

A few years ago, I heard a transportation expert in Los Angeles offer up an almost perfect illustration of the difference between local and regional goals. "When I step off the curb to cross the street and almost get flattened by a car going 50 miles per hour," he said, "that's a triumph of regional goals over local priorities."

The same can be said for economic development. Whether some economic development effort is achieving its goal depends on how you define the outcome. Very often, some project does a fine job of achieving local aims but amounts to little more than rearranging things at the regional level. Or, conversely, a project (often a big one, such as an airport) achieves regional goals but does so only by flattening a local community.

For the past several months, a rhetorical battle between the city of Anoka, Minnesota, and the Washington, D.C.-based policy organization Good Jobs First has brought this local-versus-regional conflict into view once again.

Anoka is an older community some 20 miles north of Minneapolis. It has been struggling economically since the loss of a major industrial employer, the Federal Cartridge Corp. Under the leadership of the late economic development consultant Gary Stout, Anoka used a tax- increment-financing mechanism to attract dozens of companies to its 300-acre industrial park. A major lure to the companies was free land.

There is little question that the industrial park has been a roaring success for Anoka; today the industrial park is home to at least 1,600 jobs, mostly in manufacturing. But Good Jobs First, a group that has a history of questioning the impact of deep economic incentives, looked at the Anoka situation from a regional perspective.

Using Minnesota's unusually broad public disclosure requirements for economic development projects, Good Jobs First found that all 29 companies that had been lured to the park had come from elsewhere in the Twin Cities metro area, mostly from other northern suburbs closer in to the central city. Based on interviews with the companies, Good Jobs First concluded that, while most of the companies were looking to expand, virtually all of them were planning to stay in the Twin Cities area no matter what. Their report also noted that the free land played a major role in luring them to Anoka — largely because, as one neighboring city official put it, "I don't see how companies can say no to it."

Good Jobs First concluded that Anoka had simply spent tax dollars to subsidize the relocation of companies and jobs that would have stayed in the vicinity anyway. A little less compellingly, but with impressive use of geographical data, the report argues that the Anoka relocations contribute to regional sprawl because most of these relocations came from close-in suburbs, and workers must relocate to the metropolitan fringe or commute out from central locations in order to retain their jobs.

Needless to say, the Good Jobs First report has infuriated city officials in Anoka, who have spent a lot of time defending their project as good for both their struggling city and the regional economy. No one doubts Anoka's assertion that the industrial park has revived the town economically. But on the regional front, the city's main argument is that most of the space vacated by the companies that moved to Anoka was quickly leased to other companies. In other words, Anoka's free land did not subsidize pointless business relocations to Anoka. Rather, it subsidized a needed increase in the metropolitan region's supply of industrial real estate.

This is where the regional-local conflict in economic development gets a little dicey.

If the purpose of these subsidies is to stimulate regional economic growth — well, the Twin Cities region already has the most prosperous economy of any metropolitan area in the Upper Midwest, so it's hard to believe subsidies are really needed. If, on the other hand, the purpose is to rearrange economic growth to where it is most needed within the region, then Anoka might be one candidate for a target location, but it's certainly not the only target. Anoka was struggling, but underlying the Good Jobs First critique was that there are many other communities in the region that are struggling just as much or more. They had no say in how Anoka used its subsidy, and they may be losers when Anoka wins.

Despite the city's arguments, the Anoka Enterprise Park wasn't a regional economic development effort at all. It was a pretty typical job-subsidy effort — and a successful one — by one struggling community that had access to certain financial levers with which to manipulate the regional economy, and the brains or the luck to hire a guy who knew what to do with those levers.

Whether you're an economic Darwinist or a metropolitanist at heart, it shouldn't be very surprising how this one turned out. The Anokas of this world are the towns that usually succeed at the economic development game. And why should they care whether their region has won or lost as a result of all their moves?

2000

The Rural-Metropolitan Partnership

Ever vigilant in promoting the advantages of big cities, the U.S. Conference of Mayors recently released a highly publicized report showing that metropolitan areas are the engines of the American economy.

The report goes to great lengths to show that U.S. metro economies are large in worldwide terms, pointing out not only that New York and Los Angeles have economies as big as South Korea and Australia, but even that Little Rock's economy rivals that of Kazakhstan. Most important, the mayors' report finds that the 319 U.S. metropolitan areas account for the vast majority of America's economic activity— about 85 percent of the gross domestic product.

The mayors' point is that metropolitan regions are now the foundation of the American economy. This is not exactly news, of course. But there's a crowing tone to the report, as if the mayors don't want us to miss the fact that the rural areas of our nation (which are 80 percent of the country's land area) are eating their dust. So it's worth pondering what this really means for economic development in the 21st century.

We may live in a "metropolitan world" now. But that wasn't always the case, and even big cities have often relied on a rural hinterland — usually to the mutual benefit of both city and countryside. As history professor William Cronon vividly showed in his classic book, "Nature's Metropolis: Chicago and the Great West," it is impossible to separate the 19th-century city from the rural areas with which it was intertwined. When you admire a weathered farmhouse in rural Nebraska today, remember that the wood probably came from trees in Wisconsin and Michigan that floated down Lake Michigan more than a century ago and then sat in woodpiles in Chicago before being shipped by rail out West. The rural West would not have existed without Chicago — but the reverse is also true.

Today, it's harder to make such an explicit connection between city and countryside. It's often said that the modern metropolis can function without the traditional access to raw materials — but that's an overstatement. Even regions driven by the "new economy," such as Silicon Valley, need huge quantities of raw material: wood and cement and food and silicon chips and clothes and gadgets. But they rarely get these commodities from adjoining rural areas anymore. Silicon Valley's rural hinterland isn't just California's Central Valley. It's Asia and South America and any place in the developing world able to grow, sell and ship things to the West Coast of the United States. To explain this, we're reduced to abstractions, such as the "ecological footprint," which seeks to translate the raw materials required to sustain a metro area into an acreage statistic, even though the acres are scattered across the globe.

A few rural areas in America still do a good job of exploiting their symbiotic relationship with big cities. By and large, however, it's a beauty contest. The pretty places can draw tourists and their money, especially if they are located close to thriving metro areas, while urbanites can glean "quality of life" benefits from nearby rural areas, such as when fresh fruits and vegetables are grown in the outskirts of the metropolis.

Meanwhile, the mundane locations — many of which profited in the past from resource extraction and agriculture — are being left behind.

Resource extraction has become an iffy business in the United States, although that could turn around somewhat if the Bush administration pursues its energy and resource commodity policies aggressively. And farmers must compete in an increasingly competitive global marketplace.

So the Conference of Mayors' report on metropolitan economies is not all good news. It underscores the problems created by the rapidly changing relationship between prosperous cities and their traditional hinterlands in the United States.

Of course, the mayors' conference has been working on that one, too, at least to some extent. A couple of years ago, the mayors teamed up with the American Farmland Trust to promote a combination of rural farmland preservation and urban brownfields redevelopment. That's a good idea, but it addresses only one aspect of the city-countryside relationship — land.

Rural areas need more than just undeveloped land to thrive. They require a partnership with metropolitan regions in figuring out what role rural areas in America will play in the future. If lumber from Wisconsin no longer winds up housing farmers on the Nebraska plains, then what will be the new model of how city and countryside will prosper together?.

Too often, economic developers in prosperous urban areas are so entranced by the miracle of metropolitan economic growth that they don't seem to care about their rural neighbors. But if we can get our grapes from South America and our clothes from Asia, does that mean that someday we won't need places like South Dakota? I don't think so.

2001

Sizing Things Up

Advocates of the new city-county merger in Louisville — which passed easily at the polls — said the merger was necessary to keep Louisville economically competitive.

Advocates of the San Fernando Valley's secession from Los Angeles — which lost miserably on Election Day — said secession was necessary to keep the Valley economically competitive.

Admittedly, the contexts are a little different. Louisville was a stagnant city of 250,000 people; merging with surrounding Jefferson County (population 700,000) instantly moved it from the 64th largest city in America to the 16th. Meanwhile, the San Fernando Valley is a large area of almost 1.5 million people that would have been the 6th largest city in America if it had been created; the remaining city of Los Angeles, at 2.5 million, would have fallen back behind Chicago as third.

Yet the juxtaposition of these two moves — one to consolidate and one to break apart — raises an obvious question. When it comes to economic development, does size matter? Is bigger better? Or is smaller more beautiful?

This is new territory. Americans have debated how big their municipal governments ought to be for more than a century. But rarely has the debate revolved around economic development and economic growth. Rather, from the Progressive Era forward, it's been the province of government organization junkies, who have debated which size and form of government will encourage efficiency and responsive public officials.

These days, however, the discussion is largely about economic development. In Louisville, merger advocates argued that the city was too small: Although it was a city of tremendous assets, it was overlooked on the national stage because of its size. Large corporations wouldn't take a second look. And the multiplicity of local governments led to petty jealousies and infighting over economic development opportunities. Said one economic developer: "You often spent more time negotiating with the two governments, trying to get them to agree on what we wanted to offer, and who was going to take credit and how they were going to take it, than actually negotiating with companies to get them here."

At almost the same time, advocates of San Fernando Valley secession argued that Los Angeles was too big to be competitive. A massive bureaucracy at city hall in downtown Los Angeles was seen as unresponsive not only to residents of the faraway Valley but also to businesses seeking to locate or expand there. Nearby Burbank (population 100,000) was often held up as a model proving smaller is better, especially when dealing with the entertainment industry.

In each case, however, the voters decided that bigger was better. Louisville consolidation passed in 2000 and actually went into effect this year. San Fernando Valley secession got creamed, receiving only a third of the vote citywide in Los Angeles and barely winning in the Valley itself.

But it may be that, in and of itself, the critical question is not whether the city in question is large or small. In Louisville — as in so many other older cities stagnating in population — consolidation probably makes sense as a way to attract attention and reshape its image around the idea that it is a larger place.

There is no question that the San Fernando Valley would have benefited as well from the national attention it would have received as a new city. But would a city of a million and a half really have benefited from "downsizing"? After all, if the economic development model is Burbank, then maybe Los Angeles needs to be busted into 30 different cities.

Perhaps the issue, as pundit Joel Kotkin has suggested, is not upsizing or downsizing but "right-sizing" government to be responsive both to citizens and to businesses engaged in the local or regional economic development effort.

Some metro areas have dealt with the issues of size and petty jealousies without merging. Sacramento, for example, has often talked about city-county consolidation, and for many of the same reasons as Louisville. It has a central city with stagnant population growth, a series of growing suburbs in the county and a reputation that suffers from being in the shadow of larger metro areas.

Yet even without consolidation — indeed, while further cutting up governance by creating three new suburban cities since 1997 — metro Sacramento has prospered. When it hit 1 million people a few years ago, it became a much hotter business location simply because it suddenly appeared on every location specialist's computer search.

2003

Responding

Twin Towers' Afterglow

Some 20 years ago, when my father was an aide to New York State's mental health commissioner, he would travel downstate on a regular basis for meetings at the commissioner's New York City office, which was then located on an upper floor of one of the World Trade Center towers in lower Manhattan.

The grandson of a Scottish immigrant, Dad used to spend much of the day gazing out over New York Harbor, thinking about the time more than a hundred years before when his grandfather had arrived in America as a young boy. But with his cynical view of life, my father also used to joke about why his boss's office — along with the New York offices of the governor and most other high-ranking state officials — were in the World Trade Center at all.

Like the Empire State Building before it, the landmark World Trade Center was supposed to reinforce New York's primacy as a center of commerce. But also like the Empire State Building, it came on the market during a big real estate bust, so the state propped it up financially by renting a lot of its space.

Almost lost amid the tragedy of the recent terrorist attack was the fact that the World Trade Center was one of the great economic development plays of its time — the 1960s, when big cities first began to give subsidies to private development projects. And emotion aside, the deal to build something new there will be just as important, perhaps the archetypal urban economic development decision of the early 21st century.

The World Trade Center was the brainchild of the Rockefeller brothers, who were innovators in urban economic development. David Rockefeller, the chairman of Chase Manhattan Bank, had formed one of the first business improvement districts in the nation — the Downtown-Lower Manhattan Development Association — in the 1950s, partly to protect the family's own investments in lower Manhattan, which was then going downhill.

The idea of a centralized location for businesses engaged in world trade easily captured the imagination of David's brother Nelson, the governor of New York. This was not surprising; Nelson had overseen the family's creation of Rockefeller Center in the 1930s and had aggressively used public entities to facilitate urban redevelopment all over New York State in the 1960s. (For many years, the Twin Towers were derisively nicknamed "David" and "Nelson.")

The politics and economics surrounding the World Trade Center were intense. It was originally intended to reinforce New York's status as a world port, but opposition caused its location to be moved from the Fulton Fish Market on the waterfront to "Radio Row," a seedy strip of electronics stores. The Rockefellers used the Port Authority of New York and New Jersey, a powerful public agency, to condemn the 16- square-block area and finance the construction of the towers.

New York City gave the Port Authority tax breaks that it never recouped. The towers were, of course, taller than the Empire State Building, which was then still the tallest building in the world. New Jersey complained that it wasn't getting anything out of the deal, even though the Port Authority was supposed to serve both states. And the towers opened in 1972 and 1973, just in time for the deepest recession of the late 20th century and New York's near-collapse as a world financial center. Hence the state's heavy leasing of Twin Tower space, and my father's pensive gazes into New York Harbor a few years later.

Now that the towers are gone, New York is engaged in an almost spiritual effort to decide how to combine commerce, memory, and the essence of New York in a new project on the site itself. But it's worth noting that the legacy of the Twin Towers survives throughout metropolitan New York.

The billion cubic yards of earth excavated for construction generated 23 acres of fill which were used in the Hudson River on the other side of the West Side Highway. That fill created the site for Battery Park City, an innovative mixed-used project that was a precursor to New Urbanism. To placate New Jersey, the Port Authority agreed to take over the moribund Jersey commuter trains, which were reborn as the excellent PATH system. New Jersey also got the Port Authority to build new container ports in Elizabeth. Ironically, this concession mortally wounded New York City as a port — the opposite of the original goal. But it did have the effect of consolidating high-end office space in Manhattan and industrial operations in New Jersey, a move that probably benefited everyone in metropolitan New York.

Even though he was a Republican, my dad never much cared for the Rockefellers. But I like the idea that the legacy of David and Nelson- -the brothers and the towers — remains even as the excavation of ruins continues. As for the site itself, the betting among some New Yorkers is that the final plan will be a subtle and varied design involving a larger number of smaller buildings, a greater variety of activities and careful attention to pedestrian scale. In other words, something along the lines of Rockefeller Center.

2001

A Season To Swarm

A friend of mine likes to talk about "policy cicadas" — policy ideas that remain buried for years, sometimes decades, until they suddenly surface and swarm the entire legislative process. They finally have their day.

Hurricane Katrina is a great example of the kind of storm that brings out the policy cicadas. A massive crisis, a call for dramatic action and the sudden appearance of a ton of money — these are the conditions that will bring long-buried policy ideas out into the open quickly.

President George W. Bush — not exactly a policy wonk by nature — has proposed a slew of new initiatives, ranging from the "Gulf Opportunity Zone" (a variation on enterprise zones) to "Worker Recovery Accounts"(a variation on health and retirement accounts). Mississippi Governor Haley Barbour, former chairman of the Republican National Committee, enlisted architect Andres Duany and a cadre of "New Urbanists" to tour11 devastated communities and make recommendations about how they should be rebuilt. Not surprisingly, Duany concluded that reconstruction should proceed according to New Urbanist principles.

Even the amateur policy wonks are having their day. Bloggers have proposed everything from flooding New Orleans streets with water — a la Venice — to rebuilding it as a floating city that rises and falls with the water

All of these discussions, however, really boil down to one fundamental economic development question facing the Gulf region: How should the public infrastructure be rebuilt? Despite the many different policy ideas floating around, everybody agrees that the public infrastructure has been devastated; everybody agrees it needs to be rebuilt; and everybody agrees it will be rebuilt mostly with federal money. (Indeed, Democrats have had trouble crafting a pro-active response to Katrina, largely because Republicans have usurped the traditional Democratic strategy of throwing huge amounts of federal money at the problem.)

This is where some of the policy cicadas — and even some of the crazy ideas — might come in handy. Katrina's devastation was so vast that it would seem to create a huge opportunity to rethink things. Maybe New Orleans should be on pontoons. Maybe the entire Gulf should become a kind of tax-free zone for a while. Maybe New Orleans should consider, as one wag suggested, rebuilding itself to be prosperous and ugly like Houston, rather than charming and poor.

But in the end, none of these ideas are likely to be seriously considered, and the policy cicadas are likely to go back underground with little overall impact. Natural disasters and their public policy responses, it seems, follow a familiar pattern, even in extreme cases like Katrina.

At first everyone is horrified that our society could put so many people in harm's way, so the initial impulse is to rebuild differently and move everybody somewhere else. But this "change window" is short. Over time, the accumulated effect of the televised sob stories begins to have an impact. Hundreds of thousands of people just want to have their lives back the way they were before. And gradually, the public policy responses — and the money — will begin to flow toward that goal.

After the disastrous fires in the Oakland hills in 1991, for example, California officials began to question the wisdom of continuing to permit people to live on narrow, winding streets on firetrap hillsides. In the end, the folks were allowed to stay, albeit with more fireproof houses. This same pattern has been seen over and over again in Laguna Beach and Malibu, the rich and beautiful but fire-prone oceanfront playgrounds around Los Angeles.

When hurricanes flatten South Florida or the barrier islands in the Carolinas, nobody moves. They rebuild and play the odds. When floods ravage the typical river city, few people move to higher ground. Insurance policies shift, but only gradually; there is too much public sentiment and too much private investment at stake to monkey with the status quo very much. People return and rebuild as before, trying to build stronger and more resistant to natural forces.

And so it will be in the Gulf. Sooner or later we'll stop talking about pontoons, opportunity zones and an ugly but prosperous New Orleans. We'll rebuild the levees, only we'll make them bigger and stronger in the hope that they can withstand whatever hurricanes and floods might hit in the future. We might restore a few wetlands along the way, and we'll probably build stronger buildings that can withstand winds. But in the end, New Orleans and the rest of the Gulf Coast will look a lot like it did before. And the policy cicadas will go underground again.

2005

New Rules For Hard Times

Are there enduring rules for economic development? A year ago, I would have said yes, and I would have started with a proposition that has proven very durable over the past couple of decades: Build on your strengths. But since the economic meltdown last fall, I'm not so sure. The rules of the game have changed so much, it's hard to know what will work and what won't.

Back in the 1970s, the highest-profile economic development efforts for many cities and states focused on attracting large, new businesses — often factories — whether or not the region had the labor force or other assets to support those businesses. Most of the time it didn't work out so well.

So economic developers came to an almost unanimous conclusion that the best way toward prosperity is to figure out what you have already and build on it. If your city or region is lucky enough to host a big medical-device manufacturer or biotech company, then figure out who supplies them and who feeds off them. If you've got a skilled labor force, target the industries that use it. If you've got a university, take advantage of the research that the professors undertake and students are being trained to do.

But that seems a little dated in 2009. What if your strength is creating or building something the world no longer needs as much of as it used to? Then what do you do? What if you're really good at building automobiles and parts for automobiles, as so many of our Midwestern cities are. That would be a valuable asset — if there was a market for it. But if the current recession has made one thing glaringly clear, it's that there is too much automobile manufacturing capacity in the world right now. It's not just that American cars are too expensive to make. It's that there are too few people with any reason to want one.

The conventional answer to this dilemma is that your local workers should be retrained for new jobs. But that really begs the question. What new jobs — in what new industries?

So applying "build on your strengths" to a fast-changing world economy is a whole lot more complicated than just finding an exciting new brand of car for auto-factory workers to build. It means figuring out what other economic advantages your region has, where those advantages might fit into the growing parts of the world economy, and learning how to capitalize on them in both the short run and the long run.

The most promising new thinking comes from American states and regions that are talking about how to exploit opportunities in the world's manufacturing economy to create more "high value-added" functions.

That might work. While the number of manufacturing jobs is on the decline, not only in the United States but even in China, the world's manufacturing output keeps going up. Different parts of the manufacturing process have moved to different parts of the globe, but those portions of the process where the most economic value is added are staying in the United States. According to the World Bank, the United States still leads the world — by far — in the amount of economic value added through the various stages of manufacturing. In 2004, the U.S. realized $1.5 trillion in manufacturing value added, compared with $960 billion in Japan and $740 billion in China.

In other words: Nobody in the world is increasing the supply of manufacturing jobs. But nobody in the world is better at creating wealth through manufacturing than the United States. The trick for any state or region is to figure out how to transform that wealth into new jobs, and subsequently transform those jobs into prosperity for the ordinary worker.

Not long ago, I met a smart young guy who's spent his whole life in manufacturing — both old and new. He grew up in a blue-collar Cleveland family of Middle European descent and worked his way through college on the factory floor. But he also was a math whiz and soon wound up as a graduate student at the University of California, San Diego. Now he works for San Diego biotech companies doing "data mining." But he's not mining customer databases to figure out how to sell more products. What he's doing is mining information from the precision machines that manufacture biotech products, and looking for ways to improve both quality and productivity.

In a sense, he still is a factory worker — searching for ways to create more American wealth from making things that people use. And it's unlikely he'd be all that good at his job had he never worked on a traditional factory floor to see how it works. Of course, he's in San Diego now, not Cleveland — an example of the regional imbalance in innovation in the United States. But I think he represents the future of the American economy — and states and regions would do well to spend their energy and resources learning how to combine research, knowledge, and traditional shop-floor skills to enhance their prosperity, just as one smart young man in San Diego has enhanced his own.

2009

Enriching

Growth Without Growth

Is St. Louis better off than Portland, Oregon? Are things better in Pittsburgh than in Orlando?

Well, not exactly. But according to a new Brookings Institution report, things aren't as dismal in Rust Belt metropolitan areas such as St. Louis and Pittsburgh as you might think. They are the nation's two leading examples of a phenomenon known as "growth without growth"- -places where the economy is growing strong even though the population isn't.

As for Orlando and Portland, they're examples of the opposite pattern — metropolitan areas where the population is growing faster than the national average while real per-capita income is going up more slowly than the national average.

These are the provocative results of new research by Paul Gottlieb, an economist at Case Western Reserve University in Cleveland, who measured the population growth and growth in real per-capita income in the 100 largest metropolitan areas between 1990 and 1998 to see who falls where. Most of the results were not surprising. Many thriving metros — Atlanta, Austin, Dallas, Phoenix — were above the national average in both categories. Many struggling ones, including Cleveland itself and all the metropolitan areas in Upstate New York, were below the average in both categories.

Surprisingly, however, Gottlieb found that almost half of the 100 largest metro areas fit neither category. They're either "wealth builders" — places such as Chicago, Detroit, Memphis, Pittsburgh and St. Louis — that saw income go up faster than population, or they're "population magnets — places such as Daytona Beach, El Paso, Knoxville, Orlando and Portland — that saw the reverse.

A lot of people will glom on to Gottlieb's report for their own purposes. "Slow-growth" politicians where I live in coastal California will almost certainly use it to advocate closing the door to new residents. They'll say that these statistics reveal that population growth often isn't worth the cost and that just because you stop adding population doesn't mean that you call a halt to prosperity. (Six of the 23 "population magnets" were in California, although this might have been affected by the state's deep early '90s recession.) Indeed, part of Gottlieb's motivation in doing the study seems to have been to challenge conventional wisdom. Limiting population growth doesn't inevitably harm a metropolitan area's prosperity.

But I'm not so sure that this new research supports the slow-growth argument in quite this fashion. Of the 23 "wealth builder" metro areas whose income gains exceeded population growth, the only one engaged in widespread population restrictions as a public policy goal was San Francisco. The Bay Area sure looks like a slow-growth advocate's dream: An affluent and highly educated population, growing slowly, creates one economic miracle after another, even as housing prices reach stratospheric levels.

But San Francisco was the exception rather than the rule. In most cases, the "wealth builders" were older, blue-collar places in the Northeast, the Midwest and the South: Kansas City, Little Rock, Milwaukee, New Orleans, Providence and Tampa. Population may be growing slowly in most of these cities, but the tepid rates are not because of government slow-growth policies.

What is the difference between these cities and the ones that had both low rates of population increase and little economic growth? That is, places such as Buffalo, Cleveland, Hartford, Oklahoma City, Philadelphia and Charleston, West Virginia. After all, both groups of cities have lower educational attainment and strong manufacturing bases. Even more baffling, why are some of these gritty, non-dazzling metropolitan areas doing better on Gottlieb's "growth without growth" index than supposed superstars such as Atlanta, Austin, Las Vegas and Orlando?

The answer appears to be that not adding population has some benefits. First, much of the nation's population growth in recent years has been driven by immigration, and recent immigrants pull down the overall per-capita income. And second, many of the fastest-growing metros — Las Vegas and Orlando among them — have parlayed climate and raw land into a tourism-based economy, which tends to create low-wage jobs.

The "growth without growth" champs, such as St. Louis and Pittsburgh, may experience higher levels of educational attainment and high-tech employment — more than Buffalo and Cleveland, and, at the same time, more than Las Vegas and Orlando.

In Ventura County, California, our local voters are always trying to restrict growth and send surplus residents somewhere else. I've always thought maybe it should be official government policy to ship all those extra folks to Pittsburgh and Detroit and other Rust Belt towns.

Now I'm not so sure. Maybe back in the Rust Belt, they're better off without the rest of us.

2002

Should Cities Be Venture Capitalists?

When I first got into the economic development field some 20 years ago, I heard a talk by a consultant who specialized in advising cities on business-loan programs. Cities, he warned, had to be very cautious and make sure that the business owners they made loans to were good credit risks. If there were too many bad loans, it would look bad for the city.

The consultant made a lot of sense. The political fallout from bad loans could be considerable, especially if the loans were made to political cronies. In another way, however, it made no sense at all. Shouldn't the government target business owners who could help the local economy but for some reason couldn't get a reasonable loan anywhere else? If the government is going to get into the business of providing capital for businesses, shouldn't it specialize in riskier investments?

The question, in a nutshell, is this: Should cities be bankers or venture capitalists?

Bankers specialize in low-risk, low-reward situations. They lend money to businesses and expect to get paid back in full every time. Venture capitalists focus on high-risk, high-reward situations. They don't loan money to established businesses; rather, they invest in start-ups. They know most of these fledgling businesses will fail. They expect to lose every penny on nine companies they invest in, hoping that the 10th will turn out to be Google.

It is very difficult for a city — or any government — to know how to straddle the line between banker and venture capitalist. There's little point in being just a banker, unless the city can find good business opportunities in places, such as poor neighborhoods, where conventional financial institutions are unlikely to underwrite business. But that requires great skill that, frankly, rarely exists in the public sector.

But playing the venture-capitalist role is tricky, too. The nature of the investment and the risk-reward ratio is different for a city, county or state than it is for a private venture capital firm. The government is not necessarily interested in financial return but in the creation of private-sector jobs, private-sector wealth and possibly increased tax revenue.

In the 20 years since I first heard that consultant suggest that cities should focus on being cautious bankers, things have changed. The American economy has created vast — even unprecedented — wealth. There is more capital looking for places to invest than ever before. Yet the wealth and the capital are far from evenly distributed. Most venture capital in this country comes from Silicon Valley and Boston, and not surprisingly that's where it gets invested. As a result, geographically, the rich have been getting richer and the poor, poorer. That's what's known as the "Big Sort."

So maybe it's time for cities and other government agencies to think about playing the role of venture capitalist — especially in places that are losers in the Big Sort. It's not a good idea for cities to invest directly in specific businesses. After all, cities have a wide range of responsibilities, including regulation of business, that would create conflict if cities actually own businesses. But cities, along with counties, states and regional economic development consortia, certainly could create programs that marry their own loan funds with venture-capital money.

The underlying idea, of course, is to use government loans to lure venture capital to areas without it, thus dispersing venture capital throughout the country. In this kind of a partnership, the venture capitalist would invest in a company and the city would loan the company money. The venture capitalist would seek a large financial return, and the city would be looking for other payoffs, such as jobs and local wealth creation. In this way, the city wouldn't literally be taking a stake in specific companies but, like the venture capitalist, would have to tolerate a high failure rate in hopes of hitting a home run.

Safeguards have to be put in place for the venture-capital idea to work. Cities would have to be extra-careful about cronyism. And the loans would have to be made in a strategic way, building on the region's economic assets. Otherwise such a loan program would be a scattershot effort and even successes might not yield the returns a city wants.

But as the Big Sort creates more and more inequity, cities and other governments and their agencies will have to become more creative to counteract the trend.

2007

Keeping The Wealth Close To Home

"There are no sustainable diamond mines," writes Kirk Hamilton, an environmental economist for the World Bank, "but there are sustainable diamond-mining countries."

Hamilton is the author of a hot new economic development book, Where Is the Wealth of Nations? Measuring Capital for the 21st Century. It's a book aimed mostly at the question of how poor countries with lots of natural resources can use those resources to create long-term prosperity. But these same lessons are equally relevant here — especially as the so-called "Big Sort" increasingly divides states and metropolitan areas into winners and losers.

The idea is simple: Exploitation of natural resources can create some wealth, but it can't create sustainable wealth because sooner or later the mines or the forests will be played out. In today's economy, the same is true for factories and other footloose businesses that rely on semi-skilled jobs. When the cost of labor gets too high, they'll move somewhere else — and that means a factory, like a mine, can be "played out."

The bottom line? Exploitation of natural resources accounts for only 5 percent of the nation's wealth. Production of goods accounts for another 18 percent. The remaining 77 percent is "intangible" capital — laws, education, ingenuity and so on.

The trick is to capture the wealth when and where it's created and put it to long-term use locally. Part of the reason that California is a wealthy state is that it's been doing this consistently for a century and a half. Wealth from the Gold Rush was plowed into the transcontinental railroad, which created more wealth, which endowed Stanford University, which in turn spawned Silicon Valley, which has generated vast amounts of investment capital and philanthropic wealth that is stimulating the next generation of economic growth. No matter how crowded or expensive California gets, it still draws entrepreneurs — because the wealth has been captured and invested so effectively time after time.

I'm betting that we will see this same phenomenon in the future economic prosperity of Native American tribes. All over the country, the tribes have deftly used their sovereignty to gain a competitive advantage in the gaming industry, and in the process they are accumulating wealth. Gaming may or may not be a sustainable business for the tribes in the long run, but they could recycle the current wealth into future business or economic enterprises that could create further wealth for both investment and philanthropic use. Gaming may be a short-term economic development strategy that is part of a long-term foundation for prosperity for the tribes.

The flip side of this approach is what might be called the "colonial" strategy. Investors in the centers of finance put money into natural resources and production in other parts of the world but then remove the wealth and take it back to the financial center. A century ago, British investors took advantage of the colonial relationship to extract natural resources from Africa but then took the wealth back to England with them. This is one of the reasons that London is rich and Africa is poor.

Both financial and intellectual capital accumulate in a few places — Boston, New York, Washington, Los Angeles, Silicon Valley — based partly on production and natural resource exploitation elsewhere. When the factories in these other locations are "played out," production moves elsewhere. The losers in the Big Sort are left without jobs and without wealth.

Corporate mergers have been exacerbating this problem. A century ago, even small factory towns in the Northeast and Midwest had local owners, who were both investors and philanthropists in the towns where they were located. The endowment of civic buildings and institutions from that era in such towns is impressive even today. Now, however, even if a small factory town keeps the doors open, the wealth it creates quickly flows to the other side of the Big Sort.

For the losers in the Big Sort, the solution — if there is one — lies in strengthening the place-based institutions that can't easily leave. Universities, hospitals and other such organizations are necessarily committed to a geographical area. At their best, they can both create local wealth — by serving as a base for research that could be coupled with production capacity to create innovative products — and then act as the recipient of resulting philanthropy, which can fund the next round of innovative research. In this way, even the Big Sort losers can focus on creating enough wealth so that they are Silicon Valley in a small way, rather than Africa in a big way

2007

Accounting

The Business Of Bringing In Business

A few months ago, a new secretary at Enterprise Florida — one who had recently arrived from the Florida Department of Commerce — got rush orders to photocopy some documents. Still mentally tethered to the state bureaucracy, she asked another secretary what the procedure was for making copies. "The procedure," her counterpart replied, "is to go down the street to the copy shop and make the copies." In other words, the way a private business gets things done — efficiently, without red tape.

That, in one anecdote, is the argument for turning state economic development agencies into public-private partnerships — a move recently taken by Florida and Virginia, and a trend that is likely to spread to other states. Economic development is a fast-paced world that has far more to do with business than with government bureaucracy, and economic developers have to be nimble.

So perhaps it's not surprising that the Virginia Department of Economic Development has been replaced by the Virginia Economic Development Partnership, or that the Florida Department of Commerce will disappear at the end of this year, with the state essentially contracting the work out to Orlando-based Enterprise Florida. After all, privatization has been a strong trend in local and regional economic development efforts.

A local or regional public-private partnership can only go so far, however. Only the state can deliver the really big tax breaks and business incentives, and there's no substitute for a handshake from the governor to close the deal. The ability to deliver this kind of political pop is one of the reasons governors traditionally have held state economic development efforts close to their own vests.

But now it appears that the need to build a broader base for economic development efforts at the state level has emerged as a top priority even for the governor. In both Florida and Virginia, the new entities have boards that include private- and public-sector representatives. (In Florida, the governor is chairman of the board.)

Both are working closely with local and regional economic development groups to create a more "seamless" process. And both have installed strong staff directors who have worked in both the public and the private sector. In Virginia, Wayne Sterling, who as head of the Department of Economic Development helped to snare Motorola's semiconductor plant, has moved over to the Economic Development Partnership. In Florida, John Anderson, head of the private-sector Beacon Council in Miami, has taken over Enterprise Florida. The public-private approach has been embraced by governors of both parties — Republican George F. Allen in Virginia and Democrat Lawton Chiles in Florida.

There are a host of potential problems ahead for these organizations. The question of public accountability comes up again and again, for example. In Virginia, the new Partnership is exempt from the state Freedom of Information Act so far as proprietary information is concerned, just as its predecessor was. Enterprise Florida is subject to a variety of state "sunshine" laws, but the state has been sued by a gadfly claiming that the whole operation constitutes an illegal sole-source contract.

The bigger question, however, is whether the privatization movement can withstand political pressure long enough to establish the broad base it needs in state after state. The biggest fear is what happens when the political payoff is in sight and the private entity must "hand off" business prospects to the governor to sign off on the final deal.

In Michigan, Governor John Engler and the state's business leaders spearheaded a privatization in 1994 with the creation of Michigan First. In 18 months, the group lured several thousand jobs into the state, but Engler's administration eventually brought the operation back inside state government. The privatization effort foundered on the questions of whose job it was to close a deal — and who would get the credit. "When the state people got involved, they wanted us to disappear," recalls Sue Southon, who helped start Michigan First and is now a private consultant.

Whether Enterprise Florida and its emerging counterparts disappear as well depends in large part on business leaders around the country and on state politicians outside the governor's suite. If they allow governors to use economic development for purely political purposes, the privatization movement will become just another reinventing-government idea gone bad. But if they can hang on to the private-public partnership idea long enough for it to take root, then those old Commerce Department requisition forms may soon be a thing of the past — bringing another aspect of economic development in America to maturity.

1996

The Clawback Clause

Four years ago, Georgia made a tax-subsidy deal with Alltel Corp., a telecommunications company based in Little Rock. Under Georgia's "revenue and apportionment" program, Alltel received tax breaks totaling $13.5 million over five years — one of six companies (along with Turner Broadcasting, HBO, General Electric and others) to receive such benefits.

Even at that price, it would have been a good deal for Georgia. The agreement called for the company to produce almost 800 new jobs at its Alpharetta, Georgia, headquarters. That's about $17,000 per job, but Alltel promised the jobs would pay on average more than $60,000 per year.

Last spring, however, Alltel acknowledged that it hadn't met the terms of the deal. After instituting company-wide cutbacks in 2001, the company wound up with about 135 more jobs in Georgia than it had in 1998, according to one estimate. And there was no evidence that the jobs paid anywhere near $60,000 per year.

Was Alltel simply responding to economic downturns by cutting back on its expansion plans and consolidating Southern operations in Florida rather than Georgia? Or did Georgia get taken by a company that accepted tax breaks and turned a healthy profit while welching on its end of the deal?

Either way, Georgia might be able to get some of its $13.5 million back — if it chooses to pursue Alltel under the "clawback" provisions contained in the state's tax-subsidy law. The law isn't airtight; Georgia doesn't even get a compliance report from the company unless state officials ask for one.

The state may or may not pursue a settlement. But the Alltel case is the latest example of an emerging question in economic development: If a company getting tax breaks doesn't deliver the goods, should the government agency involved demand its money back?

Clawback provisions — a term taken from tax law — are increasingly common and some givebacks are taking place. United Airlines returned more than $30 million to government agencies in Indiana last year after failing to meet its jobs goal for a maintenance hub at Indianapolis International Airport — a deal that gave the airline $300 million in tax breaks. After he was elected mayor of New York City, Michael Bloomberg rescinded a tax-break deal his company had negotiated with the city. (It was a refund steeped in irony: The subsidy was less than the sum he spent on his campaign.)

Nonetheless, enforcing clawback provisions still isn't the norm. By and large, the corporate-tax subsidy is still viewed as a one-way street in the United States.

On the surface, it makes sense to insist on a clawback. But whether it's realistic depends on how you view the true nature of a tax subsidy. It can be seen as a loan to a company: a financial liability that must be paid back if things don't pan out. Or it can be considered an investment: a financial bet by the government that the company will grow and prosper.

There's an argument both ways here. On the one hand, we're talking about tax money. It's O.K. to put that money at risk for a valid public policy objective such as economic development. But it's not a whole lot different than an economic development agency providing a below-market loan to a growing company — a risky process, to be sure, but one in which financial recourse is part of the deal. The agency loaning the money may lose it in the end if the company tanks, but it might get at least part of it back as creditors are paid off.

On the other hand, there's no way to guarantee the success of a business venture — that the markets will be there for the products and services and that contracts will continue to flow in. Given the recent history of corporate America, there isn't even any way to be sure that a large company will be managed well — or even honestly.

To take the argument a little further: It's one thing for economic developers to lay the necessary groundwork for prosperity — to provide significant pieces of economic infrastructure (airports, highways, buildings) or to try to stimulate specific parts of the economy (by encouraging networking among industrial clusters and the like). It's another thing, however, to lay a bet on a specific company. That's not economic development. That's gambling.

Clawback provisions might alter the balance of power to some extent. They could, for example, put corporate executives on alert that the government is interested in a partnership, not in giving away money.

The clauses could also have no effect whatsoever. The competitive pressures in American economic development — state against state, city against city — make it unlikely that clawbacks will become the norm rather than the exception. So let's be clear about what's going on. If the taxpayers want to lay a bet on a specific company, they can't complain about what happens to their money in a bear market.

2002

Are All Those Jobs Ever Really Created?

The torrent of announcements, press releases and gubernatorial statements on economic development keeps coming: companies expanding, companies arriving, jobs being created, tax revenue being increased — all, we're told, because of carefully crafted economic development programs and the wise use of tax dollars to encourage business investment.

Skeptics have always questioned the job-creation statistics in this gush of press releases and reports, and now there is at least one piece of evidence suggesting that the skeptics are right. A new article in the Journal of Regional Science — written by Todd Gabe of the University of Maine and David Kraybill of Ohio State University — takes a critical look at the effect of one state-level economic development program.

Gabe and Kraybill did a statistical analysis of 366 Ohio companies — existing companies, not new companies — that expanded between 1993 and 1995. Some of them received financial assistance from the state economic development program; some did not. And the results are both remarkable and remarkably clear: Providing financial incentives to existing businesses makes little difference in creating jobs. In fact, based on a regression analysis, the two professors found that, on average, businesses accepting financial assistance created fewer jobs than they would have created if they had not accepted financial assistance.

This is not news that economic development professionals want to hear, of course, and the study has been roundly criticized by state officials. But Kraybill says he also has heard from a number of economic development people who don't like the incentive game and are reassured by evidence that subsidies don't matter much. And that's not surprising, either, because the study highlighted another unfortunate reality in the economic development business: the tremendous pressure to justify one's existence by pumping up job-creation numbers.

Gabe and Kraybill not only looked at the number of jobs actually created but also compared that with the number of jobs estimated at the time the business expansion was announced. What they found was telling. The businesses that did not accept economic development incentives announced expansions averaging 45 workers — and hit the target exactly. But the businesses accepting incentives announced expansions averaging 91 workers — and expanded by only 51 workers. In other words, the businesses taking state money announced much more ambitious plans to add workers but came in at about the same level as the businesses that didn't take state money.

This is a finding that ought to send a chill down the back of every state economic development director, because it calls into question all those job-creation numbers contained in all those press releases and gubernatorial announcements and thick state reports on economic growth. Whenever State X or Governor Y announces that the state has created 10,000 or 40,000 or 100,000 jobs, those numbers are usually based on the announced estimates — not actual results.

At a time when state budget directors are looking for every dollar they can, we're beginning to see big fights over whether economic development programs are vital to restoring economic health or expendable because they don't do anything. In California, for example, the Trade, Technology and Commerce Agency has taken a 70 percent budget cut, and most economic development functions have been transferred to a tiny research section of the governor's office. There's also talk of demoting it from a Cabinet-level department. This kind of battle will go on in statehouses across the nation this year and next. Placing job creation numbers in serious question is likely to empower the budget directors in their search for more items to redline.

Gabe and Kraybill are careful to clarify that their study dealt only with Ohio, and only with expansions of existing businesses — not new businesses that have been lured to a state through economic development incentives. The results might be different in other states and might have been different for new businesses. But their conclusions certainly fit into a long line of research suggesting that money — whether financial incentives or tax breaks — is not the most important factor in determining where businesses locate and whether they expand.

Availability of labor, quality of life, proximity to certain pieces of big-ticket infrastructure such as airports — all these things matter far more than money. But they are much more difficult to quantify and much less fun for politicians to deal with. In politics, pork is a currency that everybody understands, and a well-respected measurement of whether or not you are "delivering" for your constituents. Based on Gabe and Kraybill's study, however, it would behoove our governors to focus less on delivering pork directly to the factory owners, and more on putting the pork into labor training, infrastructure and the other things that businesses really need to thrive.

2003

Pushback Time For Private Deals

Economic development is the art of using public policy, often in the form of financial incentives, to stimulate economic growth, usually in the form of more jobs and higher tax revenue. It necessarily involves strong and even aggressive use of government power. Economic developers negotiate behind close doors, subsidize private businesses and rearrange private land ownership patterns — all, supposedly, in the public interest.

But how far is too far? This is a question that always lurks around the edges of the economic development business. Recently, however, it has emerged as a front-and-center question.

The U.S. Supreme Court is pondering the "how far is too far" questioning a property rights case from Connecticut. Property owners are trying to get the high court to strike down a pretty typical redevelopment deal — one in which the redevelopment agency takes land by eminent domain from reluctant property owners and then turns it over to other private property owners who will accomplish economic development objectives. Is it in the public interest to condemn property because it isn't producing enough tax revenue or not promoting the economic development strategy adopted by the city?

Meanwhile, in Georgia, lawmakers this year debated a bill that would exempt economic development negotiations from the public records act. The Georgia proposal is part of a kind of secrecy arms race — more anymore states and localities are moving toward secrecy as a competitive advantage. The simple rationale is, "We can't give away what we're up to because then Florida would know." But the Georgia bill got a big pushback from Attorney General Thurbert Baker, who says, "Economic expediency should never outweigh the public's right to know."

Why is all this coming up now? In part, it's because some property rights advocates have morphed effectively into "economic liberty advocates," especially the Washington-based Institute for Justice, which is litigating the Connecticut case. But it may also be because competition has gotten more intense, and economic developers are pushing the envelope.

Indeed, the two instances noted above represent two separate strands of economic development. The Georgia bill is focused on classic state or local economic development: Individual businesses receive land, subsidies or other incentives. The Connecticut deal is classic urban redevelopment: A government rearranges land ownership patterns to benefit a variety of private and semi-public business-oriented entities. (In New London, a city-charter development corporation was looking to create a hotel and convention center near a recently expanded Pfizer facility.)

And this difference reveals one of the most basic conflicts in economic development: Do you try to set the table for economic growth, or do you go after individual businesses in order to get the jobs and the tax revenue you want? Either approach can work, but each requires aggressive processes that do not fit comfortably into the traditional framework of public policy.

Dealing with individual businesses necessarily involves some secrecy. Businesses are private and must use confidentiality to maintain competitiveness. Economic development offices regularly consult with businesses on a confidential basis — explaining programs and opportunities — and there's nothing wrong with that. Sometimes the offices negotiate large, one-time incentive deals with businesses. The troubling part of the Georgia proposal was that all records, including assessments of community impact, would remain secret until after ideal is negotiated.

This is where secrecy comes into conflict with the policy process. And yet, as some supporters of the bill rightly pointed out, in a competitive environment with other Southern states, what choice does Georgia have?

The Connecticut case is an inside-out version of the Georgia bill. Instead of providing subsidies to specific companies, it rearranges land ownership patterns to create new economic opportunities in a particular district. (Individual developers usually benefit in the end, of course.) This often leads to the use of eminent domain — a blunt instrument if ever there was one. Decisions to use eminent domain are often made in closed session, and sometimes turned over to private or quasi-private entities. But at least the overall redevelopment strategy is debated in public and voted on by local elected officials.

Economic development is necessarily a public-private partnership. But government agencies and private businesses are different animals, and that partnership works best when the partners do what they do best. Private businesses develop products and services. They find markets and customers, and in the process they create jobs and wealth. Economic developers often get caught up in subsidizing such activities. But government can operate most effectively by creating public policy that can serve as the foundation for private businesses to grow.

2005

Evaluating

The Cost Of Being Minor League

My hometown in upstate New York is one of the great minor-league baseball towns in America. Almost 40 years ago, the people of Auburn went down to the local ballpark, cleared the field of rocks and debris, and pooled their money to create a team. Today they still own it.

In the 1960s, the team was so good — even though it was a farm club for the worst major-league team in history — that the Saturday Evening Post published an article called "The Town Where the Mets Are Champs." Foregoing journalistic objectivity in favor of community commitment, the local sports editor — my first boss — served as president of the ball club. (When the team won, the headline read: "Auburn Wins." When the team lost, the headline read: "Auburn Plays Tonight.") Later he also served as president of the league, and today one of the league's divisions is named after him.

Now, a continent away, my adoptive hometown is struggling with the question of getting a minor-league baseball team. Only these days the question is not, "How can we do it?" but, rather, "Can we afford it?" The president of the California League has assured us that if Ventura builds a suitable stadium, we'll get a team. And a local land-owning family has assured us that their property is the perfect location for a sports complex that includes a baseball stadium; all that's required is for the city to kick in around $50 million.

It's hard to say what kind of return we'd get for this investment. A minor-league team would be fun, but it's unlikely to draw very many out-of-town fans, so the economic impact is probably small. Even the most optimistic observers concede that the city wouldn't break even operating the stadium.

And if the experience elsewhere is any indication, sooner or later the out-of-town owner will start grumbling and try to shake us down for a better deal. After all, there are always other cities that want a team. In a town where the libraries are so impoverished that they're only open three days a week, this doesn't sound like a very good investment in building a community.

Yet it's a deal that town after town throughout the country seems willing to make. Because almost all of them are farm clubs for the big league, the supply of minor-league baseball franchises is strictly controlled. Thus, like their major-league counterparts, the minor- league club owners can manipulate supply and demand to their advantage. (Part of the problem appears to be that minor-league teams have become playthings for rich fellows with major-league egos.) And like their metropolitan counterparts, minor-league towns are falling all over themselves to accommodate the owners, claiming that minor-league teams provide vast benefits for their communities.

One success story frequently mentioned is the Southern California division of the California League, where six neighboring cities in Riverside and San Bernardino counties have developed strong rivalries. Three of these towns (Rancho Cucamonga, Adelanto and Lake Elsinore) have all built new stadiums for their teams and draw well. Yet underneath the glamorous publicity lie some ugly facts.

The consensus is that Lake Elsinore paid far too much (more than $20 million) for its stadium. Tiny Adelanto (population 8,000) nearly went bankrupt servicing the debt on the ballpark and other redevelopment projects. And the remaining owners continue to play hardball with the cities. Refusing to build a new stadium, the city of Riverside (county seat of a county with 1.4 million people) recently lost its franchise to Lancaster, a town half the size. And San Bernardino, a troubled town with inner-city characteristics, has been virtually blackmailed into committing to a new stadium.

Sometimes it's hard to figure just exactly what these towns are buying that they couldn't replicate on their own without the aid of a major-league farm club. It certainly isn't community spirit or a stimulating rivalry with neighboring towns; if those factors didn't exist in the first place, the teams would fail. And it certainly isn't the excitement of a pennant race. Minor-league games are little more than simulations, providing a vehicle for scouts to watch young players under game-like conditions. Players come and go based on the whim of the major-league team, not the competitive needs of the minor- league team. Rooting for such a team is a laughable idea.

In the end, what the minor-league towns are paying for is nothing more than a designer name — the mystique of being associated with the "big club" and the ability to put that team's name on your uniforms, on your stadium and in your newspaper. This by itself is not a bad thing: Towns must constantly try to connect with the increasingly non- geographical sense of identity their residents create for themselves. But in the case of minor-league baseball, the price for tapping into that kind of identity is getting too high.

1996

What Did Washington County Buy With Intel?

Not long ago, Washington County, Oregon, a large suburban county west of Portland, received a wave of publicity for cutting an unusual deal to permit Intel Corp. to expand. Although the deal was complicated, the twist that received all the publicity was not: While committing $12.5 billion to new capital facilities in the county over the next few years, Intel actually agreed to cap new manufacturing jobs — and pay a $1,000 annual fee if it exceeded the limit.

Not since seven governors appeared on the Phil Donahue show in a desperate competition for a new auto assembly plant had an economic development story gotten so much mainstream ink. And no wonder. On the surface, the Intel deal seemed like a classic man-bites-dog story. The New York Times even quoted the state's economic development director as saying, "We aren't just interested in jobs, jobs, jobs."

Underneath the headlines, though, there's a lot more to the Washington County-Intel deal than just the "growth tax." It's true that county officials were concerned about creating too many jobs — but that was partly because Intel had already increased its employment in the county by almost 50 percent in the past five years. Furthermore, while the company will have to pay extra if it creates too many jobs, this is part of a state-sanctioned incentive that will likely save the company some $100 million in property taxes over the next 15 years.

In other words, the big news isn't what Intel is promising Washington County — it's what the county is promising Intel. And the details of the agreement reveal some important insights into how growing communities and high-tech companies must negotiate with each other these days.

The Intel pact was sealed in the context of Oregon's Strategic Investment Program, an incentive system that gives significant tax breaks to large, fast-growing companies that must make huge capital investments. Passed in 1993, when Oregon's economy was not as strong as it is now, the law was aimed specifically at the computer industry.

The program works this way: By entering into a contract with the relevant local government, a company making a huge capital investment can get its property assessments capped at $100 million. The company then must pay fees to the local government equal to 25 percent of the tax savings, up to a mandatory limit of $2 million. Beyond that, local governments can get whatever additional fees they can manage to negotiate.

With 7,500 employees in Washington County, Intel was already one of the largest employers in Oregon. In 1994, the year after the state program was passed, Intel negotiated two SIP deals with the county to lower tax assessments on $2 billion in investments in two new plants. The plants boosted Intel's employment in the county to 11,000 people, including 4,000 manufacturing workers; they also made Intel the county's largest property tax payer — exceeding Nos. 2, 3, 4 and 5 combined. Because of the likely population increase due to the Intel expansion, county commissioners decided to dedicate all of the "community service fees" generated by the SIP to local schools.

When the computer industry slumped in 1998, Intel delayed plans for more expansion. But then, early this year, the company went to county officials with a proposed new SIP contract for $12.5 billion in additional capital investment over the next few years. And this is where the Intel-Washington County deal begins to look far different from the typical economic development deal — not because of the growth tax but because of the type of investment Intel is making.

Because a new generation of computers rolls off the assembly line every 18 months, companies such as Intel must engage in constant re-tooling. The $12.5 billion was to be devoted almost entirely to this re-tooling — meaning very few new jobs would be created, but the ones already there would be retained.

So the county and Intel cut a brand-new deal under the Strategic Investment Program. Intel will pay about 30 percent more in property tax, plus the mandatory community services fee and a big chunk of money in "negotiated" fees — including the $1,000-per-job penalty if Intel creates more than 1,000 new manufacturing jobs. All told, Intel will pay the county about $110 million in new taxes and fees over 15 years.

That's a lot of money, but it's tens of millions less than Intel would be paying under any conventional property tax arrangement. On the other hand, if Intel had to pay conventional property taxes in Washington County, it would probably build new plants somewhere else in the West. So the bottom line is that both of the parties to this deal made the moves they had to make, and are deriving the benefits they need to stay healthy.

In the context of those high-stakes and crucial moves, a $1,000 "growth tax" just isn't very important. Even if it did grab all the headlines.

1999

What Gets Left Behind?

Well, it finally happened. The doomsday economic development scenario finally arrived in the city where I live: Our largest private employer is leaving town.

Everybody seems to think this proves our economic development policies have failed, but I'm not so sure. I don't think we could have done anything to avoid it. And in the long run, we may be better off without them anyway.

The company in question is Kinko's, the retail photocopying chain with more than 1,000 stores nationwide — and a large corporate headquarters about a mile from my office in Ventura, California.

Kinko's moved to Ventura 13 years ago from Santa Barbara — 30 miles up the coast — largely because the chain was growing fast and Ventura happened to have a new corporate headquarters building that was vacant because of mergers in the oil industry.

The truth of the matter is, I loved the idea of sharing my town with a nationally known company. Whenever I'm traveling — which seems to be most of the time — I usually stop by a Kinko's for some reason or another, and a while ago I even got into the habit of always alerting the local staff that I was from Ventura. I guess I figured it would keep them on their toes.

Beyond my personal feelings, Kinko's is a great corporate success story. It's a large corporation that has grown from the vision of a dyslexic founder who started a small copy shop adjacent to the campus of the University of California at Santa Barbara. And it has retained a reputation as a very good place to work — flexible hours, excellent benefits — even as it has continued to grow.

Last year, however, Kinko's founder sold his company to New York investors. And in late October, the new owners announced plans to move the corporate headquarters to Dallas. A small contingent of Kinko's employees will remain on the job in Ventura, but hundreds more will be laid off. Hardly any of them were offered a transfer to Dallas.

There's been a lot of hand wringing around Ventura about Kinko's, as everybody has attempted to use the move to reinforce their position about our local growth policies. The local newspaper, the Chamber of Commerce and our local graduate business school all argued that the Kinko's situation proves that our complicated development policies are not business-friendly. (It didn't help, of course, that the Kinko's move was announced in the middle of a city council campaign.).

But Kinko's actually turned down a $4 million incentive package that the city put together in an attempt to entice the company into staying. And the more you look at the situation, the more it looks like a classic economic development case study, where proximity and cost turn out to be more important than subsidies — for several reasons.

The first is that Kinko's has stores all over the nation, but Ventura is 70 traffic-snarled miles from the nearest full-service airport, Los Angeles International. A transcontinental trip can often take an exhausting 12 hours door to door, as I have learned the hard way over the years. In that sense, the Kinko's move was not unlike Boeing's decision to pull up stakes in Seattle and set up its corporate headquarters in Chicago.

Second is housing cost. Ventura County's median home price is nearly $300,000, and Kinko's, unlike high-tech companies in other coastal California cities, does not pay huge salaries to its corporate staff.

Finally, and maybe most important, the new boss is from Dallas.

In fact, when you think about it, it's hard to believe that Kinko's stayed in Ventura as long as it did. Why would any big corporation with a national operation choose to base itself in a remote, high-cost location — even one that has Surfer's Point and the blue Pacific just a stone's throw from the office?.

Many years ago, amid the distress in New England over the fact that Southern states were raiding the Northeast's textile mills, I heard one economic development expert from Massachusetts provide a refreshing point of view. "Those mills are headed for Mexico or Asia anyway," he said. "If South Carolina wants to rent those jobs for 10 years, that's fine with me. The sooner we lose them, the sooner we can rebuild.".

So given everything, maybe we were renting the Kinko's jobs all along. Or, perhaps more accurately, we provided a good headquarters location for the company at a particular point in its history. But then the company and the community grew apart.

Instead of beating ourselves up over what now looks like the inevitable loss of Kinko's, maybe we in Ventura should be grateful that they stayed as long as they did. And then we can get on with the business of building our economic prosperity around our community's enduring assets, rather than basing it on the kind of happenstance opportunism that led us to snare Kinko's in the first place.

2001

The Ultimate Bad Deal

There has been no more notorious economic development effort in America in recent years than the campaign by New London, Connecticut, to persuade the pharmaceutical giant Pfizer to relocate in and revitalize the city's blighted Fort Trumbull neighborhood. The New London-Pfizer deal gave rise to an infamous eminent-domain case, turned the whole question of eminent domain into a national political issue, and gave aggressive urban redevelopment efforts all over the country a black eye.

Now, however, the worst has happened in New London. Less than a decade after spending $300 million to build a big R&D plant along the Thames River, Pfizer is pulling out. And New London is forced not only to ask itself what it got for its money but also to ponder what options a city has when it lays all its bets on one company, and the company is gone after less than a decade.

Downsizing in the wake of a merger with Wyeth Pharmaceuticals, Pfizer is closing the New London facility and consolidating its research and development across the river, in Groton. New London will be left with an empty Pfizer building and the mostly vacant Fort Trumbull neighborhood nearby, which was never redeveloped as the city had hoped.

New London and the state of Connecticut spent, by one reporter's count, $160 million on the Pfizer deal. And the full cost isn't in yet.

The state and the city will continue to pay 80 percent of Pfizer's property taxes for two more years.

From Pfizer's point of view, the retrenchment to Groton makes sense. The facility there is only seven miles away by car. From the region's point of view, Pfizer's move is about as soft a blow as one can imagine. Some people will be laid off, but most will simply travel to work on the east side of the Thames River rather than the west side. Pfizer has been operating in Groton for more than 60 years. But from the standpoint of New London's local government and fiscal condition, it's an enormous blow.

Bringing Pfizer in — even at considerable cost — did make some sense in the beginning. A faded 19th-century city surrounded by seaside affluence, New London had reason to hope that spending money and political effort to direct investment to older parts of the city might revive them. Certainly nothing else had solved the problem.

So New London delivered an old carpet factory to Pfizer. At least partially at Pfizer's request, the city condemned most of the adjacent working-class neighborhood around Fort Trumbull in hopes of attracting ancillary development. Suzette Kelo, a resident of the neighborhood whose house was condemned as part of the project, sued on the grounds that taking a citizen's property in this manner for private development, rather than public use, was an improper exercise of governmental authority. The city defended its actions all the way to the Supreme Court, and ultimately prevailed, but the decision was so unpopular among New London residents that local leaders were reluctant to use their newly won power.

What did New London buy with all this money, hassle and bad publicity? Is it possible that the whole exercise somehow laid a foundation for long-term prosperity? That's a hard case to make.

Unlike other locales that attract and later lose a plant, New London did not get a skilled new labor force or a chain of suppliers. Those were already present because Pfizer had been across the river in Groton for decades. Nor did New London ever get the "urban village" that it was expecting to create around Fort Trumbull, which could have attracted other investment. Pfizer wanted the urban village, but it doesn't exist, partly because of the city's caution in the wake of the Kelo controversy.

Just about the only thing New London has left for its money and effort is the Pfizer building itself — which is still owned, at least for the moment, by Pfizer. "Basically, our economy lost a thousand jobs, but we still have a building," Councilman Robert Pero told one newspaper reporter. Then he added, "I don't know who's going to be looking for a building like that in this economy."

It's always a tough call in economic development whether to invest in existing economic infrastructure or go after the home run with the big company that can turn your town around. New London went for the home run. That was understandable; the city had been on the skids for decades and Pfizer represented a quick victory. In the end, however, the New London story reaffirms what may be the most important lesson in economic development: The measure of success is not in the company you attract but what you've got when the company leaves.

2010

About The Author

One of America's leading commentators on urban planning and economic development, William Fulton currently serves as Mayor of Ventura, California.

Mr. Fulton is the author of several well-known books, including *The Reluctant Metropolis: The Politics of Urban Planning in Los Angeles*, which was a *Los Angeles Times* best-seller; *Guide to California Planning,* the standard textbook on urban planning in California; and *The Regional City: Planning for the End of Sprawl*, co-authored with Peter Calthorpe. He was the founding editor and publisher of the periodical *California Planning & Development Report* (www.cp-dr.com). He has written for *Governing* magazine (www.governing.com), for which the columns collected in this book were written, since it was founded in 1987.

In his professional life, Mr. Fulton is a Principal with Design, Community & Environment (www.dceplanning.com), a California-based urban planning firm, and a Senior Fellow at the School of Policy, Planning, and Development at the University of Southern California.

A native of Upstate New York, Mr. Fulton served as the Chair of the Planning Commission in the City of West Hollywood, California, in the 1980s. He was elected to the Ventura City Council in 2003 and became Mayor in 2009. In recent years, Ventura has gained a reputation as one of the most innovative cities in California. Among other things, Ventura has adopted an all-infill general plan, invested in a high-tech venture capital fund to attract business startups to the city, and established a benchmarking system to track the city's progress against goals.

www.ingramcontent.com/pod-product-compliance
Lightning Source LLC
Chambersburg PA
CBHW072127270326
41931CB00010B/1697